Wholesale Seafood: The Good, the Bad, the Ugly

True Life Stories of Richie the Fish Fullo

Richie the Fish Fullo

NEWMAN SPRINGS PUBLISHING
320 Broad Street
Red Bank, NJ 07701

First originally published by Newman Springs Publishing 2023

ISBN 978-1-68498-552-4 (Paperback)
ISBN 978-1-68498-553-1 (Digital)

Printed in the United States of America

To all my readers, this book is based on all real people, real actions, and all true stories. Some of the names of characters are changed to protect their identity. Some of the locations are also changed to protect them also from misinterpretation. There may be some wording and stories that may not be appropriate for minors. There may be some language that may be controversial, but it is not meant show any demeaning or prejudice of any race, color, or creed. This book is full of adventure, happiness, sadness, and most of all, daring and crazy adventures. This book's stories and locations take place from Maine to Florida. Most of the highlights were located in New Jersey and New York. This story is based on an average middle-class family where the oldest son was the black sheep of the family. He grew out of control each year and became more aggressive in certain areas. I hope everyone enjoys this reading and can share my happiness and accomplishments.

This book is dedicated to my dear dad; rest his soul in peace.

I would like to thank the following for their help:
Joseph O. Holmes
Brooklynyte 4 ever
Maryjo Defranco
Neil Henn

Contents

Description of Characters

Father: My dad was a stocky 5'9" bald-headed man who had hands that were rough like sandpaper ridden with calluses. He was a man of very few words and quite stubborn in his ways. Artie drank occasionally and smoked quite often. His life's passion was fishing. Arthur was so serious about his profession that many times it took precedence over his family life. He was not around during much of his children's social activities. Nevertheless, he worked very hard and provided the family with all their needs. Later in his life, he became a compulsive gambler, which destroyed his health, finances, and family life.

Mother: Yolanda was a petite woman. She had a heart of gold and not a bad bone in her body. She did everything imaginable for her four children to enjoy every opportunity possible. Yolanda made sure her children ate properly and healthy, had adequate medical and dental care, and many times had to play the role of mom and dad. She tried to be a wonderful wife but was not appreciated. In her later days of life at ninety-three years old, Mom's memory started to deteriorate. She became manipulated by her younger daughter. The younger daughter, to this day, never left her nest.

Yolanda's Mom, (Grandma) Maria: Maria was a short, heavyset Italian immigrant from Sicily. Her wardrobe left a lot to be desired. She did not have many of these dresses or whatever you want to call it. She lived in America for many years and could not speak one word of English. I have never met Yolanda's dad, Joseph (Grandpa). I have never met Arthur's mom, (Grandma) Rose either.

Arthur's father, (Grandpa) Siegfried: He was a short, stubby old guy with glasses. His clothing was plain and simple. He would have this cigar dribbling from his side of his mouth.

Arthur's only sibling, Ellen, was married to Harry and had two children, Robin and Steven. Aunt Ellen was a very good person; her downfall was she was very overweight.

Harry, on the other hand, was the complete opposite. He was very trim. He was a very quiet and obedient guy, basically like the dog. My aunt had him trained well.

My cousin Robin was a little on the heavy side. She kept to herself.

My cousin Steven was very quiet and shy. He was very close to his father as a young boy. Yolanda (my mom) had many siblings. She had three sisters and four brothers.

I am giving brief descriptions on the siblings. The oldest sister was Mary. She was married to Jimmy and had one son, Rudy. Aunt Mary was quite petite and your perfect Italian wife who did everything for Uncle Jimmy, who was very boisterous and demanding, especially when he had a couple of glasses of homemade Italian wine.

Rudy my cousin was a gem. There are a few paragraphs about him later in the book. This guy, to this day, is an ace, an incredible guy.

My aunt Anna was also petite. She was very boisterous and was a real pain in the ass—at least for me.

My uncle Sollie was a very well-rounded guy. He was very knowledgeable about many things.

There was cousin Bobby, who was of Rudy's age bracket, and they were actually neighbors growing up in Brooklyn. He was very quiet, and there are also a few chapters about his misfortune in life.

Then there was my cousin Jane, who grew up contracting polio, which was her cross to bear her entire life. She had met an angel out of the sky. Later on, they got married and had two children, then her angel passed away at a very young age.

My aunt Barbara was my favorite aunt; she was also my godmother. She had always lived very close to us growing up. Barbara and my mom were very close. They were best friends growing up and in adult life. Aunt Barbara was very good to me; she treated me like the son she never had. She did so many things for us when we were kids.

My uncle Joe was a little stern. He was a merchant marine from Kingspoint and was very tough. Unfortunately, he had four children and all were girls. He really wanted a son in the worst way.

Among my four cousins, Linda was always a little snobby and thought she was God's gift to the world, and to this day, she hasn't changed. She is the worst.

Carol was the second oldest. She was more pleasant than Linda.

Then Nancy was my age. We went to school together. This was a terrible thing for me because my mother used to compare notes with Aunt Barbara about our school work. Nancy was always bringing books home and had homework. I, on the other hand, never brought books home or had homework. Nancy was very quiet until she got out of school and headed to California, She changed completely, a complete looney tune. We believe she was one of many stunt acts in Hollywood.

Then the last cousin was Maryjo. In my opinion, she was the only good one. She married a really nice Italian guy and had a family of three children.

Her brother was the first Johnnie. He was married to a lady whose name was Suzie, who was previously married with a son named Robert, who later on made it to Hollywood and was a professional actor. They had two daughters together.

Kathy and Suzie were raised in the 1960s through the beginning of drugs, alcohol, and rock 'n' roll. They got mixed up in the wrong crowds. That's all I know; I was very young.

Next was Charlie. He was a quiet guy. My other uncles always used to tease him. He was married to Sarah, who was ridiculous with her actions and had stinky perfume and lipstick that would always end up all over your face. Our parents would always make us kiss our aunts when they came over. It was a nightmare dealing with the lipstick all over the face and the stinky perfume and getting squeezed like a wet towel.

There were two cousins. Victor was a lot older and was very polite and well-groomed. One family mystery was he never had a girlfriend even to this day. Makes you wonder which team he was playing for.

The other cousin was Marie. She was totally fucked up. There is no other way to even try to explain it. She was mentally disturbed. Her parents refused to accept it and find help for her. I will give you two examples. One time, we went away on a weekend to Wildwood Crest and stayed over in a motel. The next morning, us kids went out to the pool, and Marie decided to make a shit in the middle of the pool. Well, the manager was so pissed off he had to empty the pool, change the filters, then he threw us out of the motel. The second time, we went fishing, and we had live killys and fresh, raw squid strips. It took one minute before Marie grabbed the raw squid and was eating it, then she started putting the live fish in her mouth and was eating them until we stopped her and made her spit it out. She hence inherited the name "Marie from Brooklyn."

Then there was another brother, Carmine. This one had post-traumatic stress disorder from the war. He became an alcoholic, and it was hard for him to keep a job and was a lost sheep. He actually was thrown off a roof of a building and died.

The last was Sammy. He was a good person; he is mentioned later on in the book. He was married to Ally.

There were three more cousins, Ralphie, Joseph, and Salvatore.

DAILY NEWS

NEW YORK'S HOMETOWN NEWSPAPER

50¢

Thursday, March 30, 1996

SOMETHING FISHY

Massive arson probe in Fulton Fish Market blaze

SEE STORIES PAGES 2 & 3

Chapter 1

My father and mother are both American-born citizens. My father was born and raised in Brooklyn, New York. My mother was born in lower Manhattan in the Bowery section (little Italy). My mom's mom, Grandma, came over from Sicily with her sisters. My mom's dad, Grandpa, also came over from Sicily. They both met in lower Manhattan and got married. My mom came from a very large family three sisters and four brothers. My mom was the baby of the family. She had a tough time growing up with most of the brothers went off to war, and her sisters started getting married. Money was an issue since they were immigrants, and neither her mom or dad could only speak Italian. They were limited to the work they can do. It was also  the Depression time when Grandpa had to do what he had to bring food to the table. The stories were he would be selling fruits on the street corner. My mom could only speak Italian as a child for the longest time until she learned English with the other children in school. She had a limited childhood due to lack of money. She lived between Jewish, Chinese, and Italians. As she reached her teens, her family moved to Brooklyn. She graduated high school there. She started working for Bamberger's department store in New York City. In her twenties her dad had passed away. Some time had passed, and she met my dad. I will continue this part and go deeper once you have been filled in on Dad's history.

My dad came from a very small family. He was born in Brooklyn, New York, and had an older sister. His mom was Austrian/German, and his dad was the same. His mom had left to go to England for safety and peace from the rise of the Nazis. She then fled to the United States. His dad had also left for the same reasons and ended up in the United States. His mom also left because she was in a bad marriage and had to get out. My grandmother's name was Rose, and my grandfather's name was Siegfried. They met in Brooklyn and decided to get married. They had two children, Arthur and Ellen. When my dad was twelve, Rose passed away. She was very young, in her early forties. She came down with some strong disease that they did not have any cures or medicine for. My dad was left without a mom at twelve years old, and his father raised him. His sister had gotten married to a guy named Harry. Harry was very different type of guy.

He was very obedient like a little puppy dog. He worshipped Ellen, and later on, they had two children, Robin and Steven. They lived in the downstairs level of his brother's house. Later on in the book, you will hear more about Harry, Robin, and Steven. My dad and grandpa went to live with her. Time went on, and Dad finished high school. He then took a liking to the ocean. He worked down at Sheepshead Bay, Brooklyn, on the party boats. His dad met a woman, and he married his wife number two, Helen. One day, one of the guys on the pier asked that if he would like to work on his commercial fishing boat. The money would be big, and he would have steady work. He swept that opportunity up. He went out on that commercial boat and saw a new life in front of him. He had more responsibility and very hard work to deal with. That twelve-year-old boy without a mom to guide him learned to survive at a young age. He finished and graduated high school. At eighteen, he was ready for anything. He fished for days at a time and horrendous weather and high seas. This man does not have any fear of the seas. He was on a boat that capsized and sank in a storm. He managed to survive and swim to safety. This story is very true and was documented by the local newspaper for verification. He fished on many different boats for fish and scallops. The stories this man told me about his adventures are unbelievable. When he worked on the scallop boats, there were so many scallops to open his wrists would swell up. There were Porgy trips out of Montauk, Long Island. They had caught so much the boat was overweight. They had to shovel some of the fish overboard. This guy was a real fisherman; he led that wildlife. They would pull into port, unload their catch and have a wild night drinking with woman and his fishing buddies, Austin and Freddie. Freddie actually became my godfather and his best man in his wedding.

Time went on, and Artie's wildlife and hard work were catching up. He and Freddie went to Freddie's apartment in Sheepshead Bay, where he lived on the bottom floor of this two-family rowhouse with his wife and his two kids. On the top floor, my aunt Anna and uncle Sal lived. My mom was visiting them. This is how Mom and Dad met. They started dating. Things started getting serious; Dad really fell for Mom. It came to the point of decision time: Shit or get off the pot. Then he was given alternatives. "If you want to marry me, you must give up commercial fishing." This statement dramatized my dad for a while, and he gave up his wild and crazy commercial fishing life. Then they got married and moved out to West Orange, New Jersey, and rented out one of the apartments in the two-family home my aunt Barbara and uncle Joe bought. One year later, I was born, the beginning of a new generation, new ideas, crazy adventures, and a new way to do business.

Dad's first adventure was in the local area of West Orange. There was a fruit and vegetable store there, and he had taken the opportunity to rent out a section of the store to sell fresh fish. This did not work out for any length of time. There was not much foot traffic, and the owner of the food store had sticky fingers. He was helping himself to my dad's cash register and his

product. The next opportunity came up for a retail fish market located in downtown Montclair on Bloomfield Avenue. There was quite a difference from his first adventure into retail. He was his own boss and had control of his security, money, and product. He had his own little pickup truck where he would venture down each early morning to the Fulton Fish market in lower Manhattan. My mom often would help him in the store and bring me along as an infant in a carriage. He also had some employees. Business started to grow, and so did Dad's equity. He began to save some money. Like they say, money makes money. He used that philosophy and reached out and started doing some wholesale business. He had picked up some local restaurants, which he supplied.

As a few years passed, this Italian neighborhood changed. It started to get darker, and the Italians were moving out. His business was changing. He was selling more Porgy's and Whiting. He also had to hire a black man to work with him part-time. This man was very nice and educated. He was a local policeman who worked part-time for Dad.

In the early sixties, the Newark riots broke out, and there was mayhem. There was looting, vandalism, fires, and explosions. Lower Montclair, which is very close to Newark and has now a high percentage of black residents became a branch of the riots. Dad's windows were broken, and the store was slightly damaged. He was protected by his worker, who was a full-time police officer. The troublemakers and rioters backed off his store. My dad did not feel comfortable being there. Mom and I were not allowed at the store anymore.

Time went on, and Dad heard a rumor of a very successful retail market going up for sale in upper Montclair. Upper Montclair was a totally different animal than lower Montclair. His clientele would exist of movie stars, major athletic stars, and major owners of corporations. These people, at this time in history, had their own private housekeepers and butlers and were members of the high-end country clubs. Dad did not have to think too long. This was a no-brainer. He knew this would change everyone's life. His only thought was, *How and where can I get this money to buy this store?* Fortunately, the people that were selling the business were retiring down to Hollywood, Florida. They were a nice couple, very understanding and were willing to work with Dad. They made arrangements, and Dad made a hefty down payment and each month would send them a nice, fat check. Dad was able to sell whatever he could get for his Lower Montclair store. He then relocated to the Golden Rule located on Bellevue Avenue, Upper Montclair. Within no time, Dad adapted to this new environment. He was selling high-end fish he had never dealt with before: Florida red snapper, pompano, and Alaskan salmon. He had only sold local fish. Business was getting better every day. He was then able to grow his wholesale business. Dad worked harder and harder. He then saved money to buy our first house. It was located on Forest Hill Road W., Orange. He was so proud. My brother was born. Afterward, we moved in. My dad still had his car, which he brought with him from Brooklyn, New York. It was a DeSoto. It was a beautiful car. Then one day, he started to go to work. Something went wrong. We smelled smoke, and Dad came running in to call the fire department. Yes, the car caught fire. He was very sad, and my mom and I looked out the window in amazement.

Chapter 2

Sometime in the summer of my eighth birthday, I became more aggressive. I wanted more things, my allowance wasn't cutting it, my parents did not want to spoil me; they made me earn it. I was getting older and driving Mom crazy.

It was time that I would work with Dad on Saturdays. I grew up in this middle-class neighborhood. It was a mixed ethnic area. There wasn't one group of ethnicity greater than the other. Actually, looking back, I would classify it as totally American. There were few to no immigrant families or black families present. I adapted very well. I had many friends on the street and some from school. We 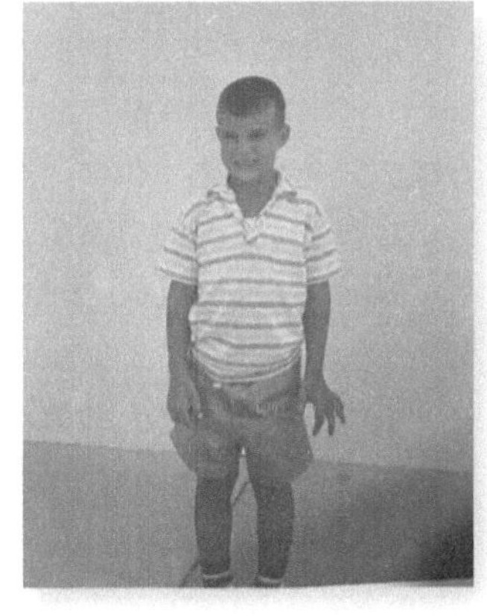 would walk to school and back each day. There were no buses, and Dad was already out of the house in the wee hours of the morning. He would purchase his fish. Mom did not drive yet. It seemed like she was a housewife, always pregnant. To clarify that statement, there were four of us: two boys and two girls, all two years apart. My mom and dad gave us free range where we were to play and walk. Times were different; there were no pedophiles, kidnapping, children trafficking, etc. We did not need to tell them where they could find us. They knew our habits and play places, so it was predictable where we were. Across the street, there was a large wooded area where we would play. I would also play at the neighbors', my friends' backyards, and mind, I became quite rugged playing and running all the time.

I will fill you in a couple of events that were memorable in my early youth. The first one was when I became the big brother to my brother. He was playing with one of my neighborhood friends, and my friend attacked my brother for no good reason. I then lost it and went after my very good friend Vincent and gave him the beating of his life. He was bloodied, etc. That night, I knew all hell was going to break loose. It did. Vincent's father walked out to our house rang the bell and told my parents what happened to his son. My parents then told him your son deserved it for picking on a little boy. I was then summoned not to play with Vincent anymore.

Second story, I lived two houses away from my best friend Jimmy Ratner, whose dad was a dentist. Every day, his father would bring him home packs of Tops baseball cards. Of course I became jealous and pestered my father to do the same. Each day, we would wait for our fathers to come home with our treats.

The next story with my friend Jimmy—we were in his basement and in the bathroom there was a towel rack. I then tried to do a pull-up on the rack and ripped it out of the wall. I have no idea what happened. All I know was he was screaming that his parents would kill him and now he was going to kill me. He ran into his garage and grabbed the pitchfork and then, as hard as he could, jabbed me in the ass like he was jabbing a haystack. Let me tell you, I saw fucking stars. My ass was bleeding from the pitchfork marks. If he would have gone a little higher, he would have hit my spine. I probably would not be writing this book now.

The third memorable story was in our backyard. It was very limited to play in; it was divided on both sides with flower beds. The back was a shaded cooler area with trees. We tended to go to the back area because we would always get bitten by the king, queen, and yellowjacket bees. Damn, those bites used to hurt and swell our arms up. Getting back to the story about the back area, I decided to make it into a jail cell with a bathroom. We would play a game, and the loser would  have to go to jail. We would also pee outside in a makeshift bathroom until my mom discovered what was going on, and then the jail game ended. Well, getting to the point, one day, my mom went out somewhere, and I was playing with my friends. I needed to go to the bathroom number two in the worst way. I was desperate. The front door area was with square glass panes, which was part of like an entrance, which I guess could be called a vestibule before the front door. I had the key for the front door but not the hallway door, which was locked. With no delay or thought, I immediately lost it and began kicking in the glass panes to gain entry. I knew after that stunt there would be hell to pay when Dad came home. Rest assured I was correct. I received a nice beating, and we set up a weekly payment plan from my allowance to fix the windows.

On another note, my younger brother and I always would be fighting or playing rough. My mom did not have it easy. We were quite energetic and caused a lot of problems wherever we were. Here is an example in those days. Doctors made house calls. The doctor would come to the house and we would be hiding so we wouldn't have to face getting injections or take the horrible medicine. Often, my brother would get hurt in the house and need to go to the hospital.

We were terrible when we went shopping. One day, I even got my leg caught in the escalator at E. J. Corvette's Department Store. I have a nice butterfly stitch, which left a scar forever. We were bad kids, but we learned. We were disciplined the good old-fashioned way. Some days, we drove my poor mom so crazy she would call Dad at work and pester him out of frustration. Then that night, when we heard him come home, we would hide under the beds. He was determined to give us what we deserved. He would pick up the bed, and then it was over, *bam wam*. Hopefully, we would have learned, but no, we didn't.

One of the last memorable stories from the forest hill road era was Dad was doing well in business; he bought a brand-new black Coup Deville Cadillac. This was his baby. Every Sunday, religiously, he would take it to the car wash. One Sunday afternoon, we were playing in front of the house, me and my brother and cousin Steve. My friend Craig Cordasco was walking up the street, and he was a movie star in his youth. He was a pretty boy—perfect body no scratches, no imperfections, etc. He would make commercials. His most famous movie was *The Green Beret*.

He would always brag about himself, etc. So I bragged about our beautiful car. My cousin Steve and I were playing, then we saw Craig grab a plate of leftover TV dinner out of someone's garbage and threw it all over Dad's toy, the Cadillac. I was always getting into trouble, so my first instinct was to kick the crap out of him. I didn't. I ran to tell my father what happened he came out and saw his car. The first words out of his mouth were "Get him!" That's all I had to hear. I was like a German Shepherd attack dog. I ran after him and beat the living daylights out of the pretty boy. His body and face were damaged. He would be out of the movie business for six months. My cousin couldn't stop laughing after this incident.

Please don't take the stories to mean we were devils. There was also the good boy. I would walk to church every Sunday, and on Saturday, we would go into the scary, dark confessional booth. My school grades were fine, not great but good. We were raised Roman Catholic children. My parents did not have or teach us any prejudice against anyone. My uncle Sal was a very bad influence on me and my brother. I was innocent and became friends with a black boy in school. His name was Stephen. He was like everyone else. My uncle caught wind of this and wouldn't stop making fun of me with many racial slurs.

This was not the only thing. Back in the day, Converse sneakers were the in thing. I had bought a red pair, which looked really cool until my uncle ridiculed me and said "Red is for girls, and you are a sissy." The final thing he did to me was when I decorated my bedroom, probably at the age of eleven or twelve. I put a stylish long vase with a fancy flower arrangement. Well, he didn't let up on that. It is examples like this how children are formed in their ways of thinking and actions.

Childhood Embarrassments

One of many of my childhood embarrassments was when I was at school; it was recess time. We were outside on the playground. Some of us were playing ball. I had taken a break from running around. I was hot and sweaty. I took my winter jacket off; the weather was getting warmer. I was sitting on a inclined hill. I put the jacket behind me. I was sitting just so still like a statue.

All of a sudden, out of nowhere, I felt the back of my pants and my shirt get wet. My jacket was soaked. Lo and behold, I saw a giant dog that was lifting his leg toward me, finishing peeing on me and my articles of clothing. He had mistaken me as a tree with hair. I did not know how to explain this episode to any of the kids because I would be the laughingstock of the school. I was also embarrassed to tell the teacher. Lucky for me, no one saw the incident. Someone on the way to the classroom screamed out, "What is that smell?" It definitely smelled of piss. I then managed to hide my jacket and go to the boys bathroom' and tried to dry my clothes with those cheap brown paper wipes. I could not wait for that day to end.

This story is incredible. Back in childhood, I used to be

so fresh I would tell my Aunt Barbara what she had to buy me for Christmas. She would always tease me and say that bad boys didn't get good presents. They received charcoal and garbage because they were not good boys. So lo and behold, that day finally came at her house. Christmas was such a special, wonderful time. All our families would get together—aunts, uncles, cousins—and eat unbelievable food and all homemade Italian cookies. One Christmas, they went as far as to rent a Santa Claus on a sleigh pulled by horses coming up the street in a snowstorm with our presents. What an unbelievable event. Well, back to my present. All the kids opened their

gift; there was so much joy and happiness. I was the last one to receive my present. I opened my present. Inside was a box of egg shells, coffee grinds, and garbage. Also, there was a note to check my stocking. I did; inside was charcoal. Let me tell you my face dropped to the ground of embarrassment and sadness. I was so, so mad. I ran off crying.

Summer Home

My dad was doing so well in business he decided to buy a summer shore house in Beach Haven West, South Jersey. This was a new development that was actually a new town. It was swamp lands along the lagoons that was developed into streets and houses. We had a beautiful home on the lagoon. I think he paid nine thousand for this new construction. It was unbeliev- able the way things went up. He had a boat parked in the back, and we would go fishing on the weekend when he came down. He left our family with my aunt Barbara's family during the week at the house. He and my uncle Joe would come down on weekends. We would catch bush-

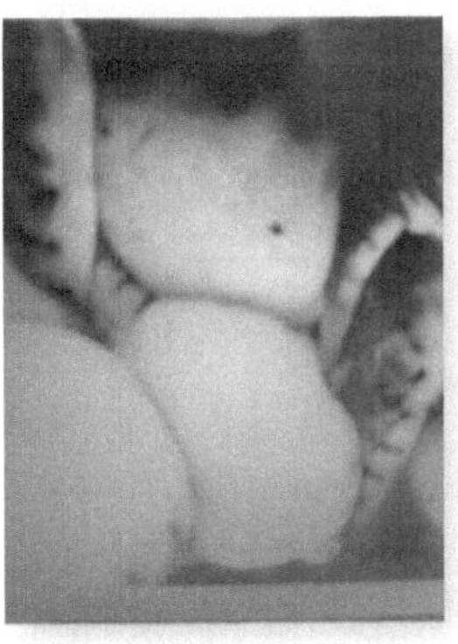

els of crabs and all kinds of eels in the lagoon. When we went fishing, we would catch all kinds of fish and a lot of them. Things were very different than now. Now you can't catch a third of what you caught back then. One memorable time I can never forget. We were in Barnegat Bay blowfishing. All of a sudden, there were thousands of blowfish surrounding the boat. We put our poles in the water and were catching three at a time.

Then on the boat we had a pole with a net on the end, and I said "What the hell?" and then Dad was filling up the net with the blowfish. The entire boat floor was covered with these fish. It was the most incredible sight I ever saw. The reason they are called blowfish is that they blow themselves up like little balls and you can actually bounce them on the floor. These fish are also known as chicken of the sea. Once you fillet them, they look like little pieces of chicken, and fried up, they are so sweet.

Dad's business kept growing bigger and bigger, and so did his expectations. He decided to build this big dream house in West Orange from scratch. Time went on, and there were some delays with the house. We were supposed to move in for the summer. Well, that didn't happen. To make things easier for Mom and Dad to try to make this move happen, they sent me and my brother off to summer  sleepaway camp in the Hamptons, Long Island. Let me tell you, we were not ready for that. There were all sorts of characters there. I again was the protector for my younger brother. We both begged our parents not to leave us there. We tried escaping many times. It was like a concentration camp with guards, strict rules, and bugles to wake you up and to get you to sleep (lights out). Bad experience, not recommended.

Summer was over, and we began our new school and home. We had to make new friends and learn new shortcuts to go and come home from school. I had to make a name for myself. I participated in some sports in school. I basically started to fit in. My school grades were not the greatest. For some reason, teachers would always mark off my report cards with "attitude needs improvement." Well, one day, one of my teachers, Mr. Hackess, who was a flaming faggot—in those days, that was not common—pulled a real power play. He demanded my father come in on Thursday morning for a parent conference about me. My mom and I told him that was not possible because of Dad's job. He insisted it would be Dad, not Mom. If Dad couldn't come, I would be expelled from class until he could make time to come in. Well, I knew what this meant: big troubles and a good beating for me. Dad's busiest day was Thursday morning. For him to leave his business was a major sacrifice on his part. Well, the teacher spoke a lot of shit to Dad; he also commented that I would be a failure in life. I have a very poor attitude. Yes, my ass that night was as red as the apples in the refrigerator.

In the summertime, we were off from school every year. We would take a couple of trips to the Fulton Fish market in Manhattan with Dad. That would consist of an early evening of sleep and waking up about 2:00 a.m. We would drive over to the store go inside check everything was running and head off in this very large international box truck. The ride to the market was like writing on an amusement ride. It was rocky and shaky. The only sound was standard; the radio was only allowed on one channel, 1010 Wins, the same shit over and over on the way there and back. Let's not forget the cigarette smell. We finally reached the Holland tunnel; there were signs of life. We saw many other fish trucks on their way also. We got out of the tunnel and went downtown; it was quite a ride, all very large government buildings and cobblestone roads. It

seemed like we would never get there. There was a traffic light it seemed like every other block. Voila, we finally arrived. We drove down Peck Slip to our designated parking spot, which was called Stephanie. We pulled into the lot and started to park the truck. These trucks had to be lined up like soldiers in a row. There was this big guy named Benny dressed with overalls and

a hook on his shoulder and a big, fat half-smoked cigar hanging out of the side of his mouth. He started to direct us into the parking spot. We then got out of the truck, and Benny greeted us, "Good morning, Artie. You have your helper, little Artie."

I replied, "No, my name is Richard," and I brought him to the front of the truck on the hood. Dad had our names painted on—Richard, Jimmy—I guess that was a cool thing to do in those days. While we started our morning journey, there were wood boxes of fish piled higher than I could see. There were puddles of stinky fish water all over. It was two streets long, and there were two different market houses. There were even boats that would still show up in those days. I was so amazed at all these dead fish. Where did it all come from? Day after day, I just couldn't imagine.

Well, it was now about 4:00 a.m., and Dad wanted to get first pickings of the good stuff. It started getting busier; more buyers were coming. I would follow behind him closely so I wouldn't get lost. Dad was well-liked in the market. He got along with everyone and played by the rules. The rules we will get into in a later chapter. Most of the companies he used to sell fish to when he was a commercial fisherman. Some of the guys were from Brooklyn where he went fishing.

It was about 5:30 a.m. Now most of the buying was done. Now it was chow time. This was one of the best parts of the trip. There were two choices—the Paris bar or Dirty Ernies—pick your poison. Well, at my younger age, Dad did not bring me to the Paris bar. There was a full bar; they served breakfast. It was  not a place to bring a kid. A lot of the workers and some buyers were doing shots, and some got really sloshed. There was a lot of cursing, and I seem to remember there were some women there also, probably some ladies of the night. Well, we made it to Dirty Ernie's, and they had a big, juicy roast beef and a ham displayed in the window as you walked by. Inside was a counter that was on a slant. If you didn't place your cup and plate just so, it would slide. Inside were two women behind the counter working with Ernie, nicknamed Dirty Ernie. Place was a shithole, but you never had such a roast beef sandwich like that. Ernie never smiled or laughed; the two woman would just do their jobs and try to ignore the rude comments from the fish-monger's. They didn't have to worry about the guys hitting on them because it was known they were dykes. After breakfast, we would check the truck, see what was not delivered, and finish our buying. We would pull out of the market at about 7:00 to 7:30 a.m. Some of my favorite stops at the market was the Meyer Thomson smoke house. They would smoke fresh cod, which was called *fininhaddie*, and smoked whiting. You could savor that delicious smell blocks away. My next favorite spot was inside the little booth office at Atlas Foods. They would have the best playboy centerfolds decorated on the walls.

As time went on, Dad's business was very demanding. He had some customers that required a certain brand of imported shrimp. They would not be available at all times. The ship would come into port and then get distributed to different companies. Well, the shipment came into Atlas Foods on Peck Slip. Dad had finished his buy-ing and drove the truck up Peck Slip to pick up the shrimp from Atlas. They loaded the big international box truck up with a hefty load of these expensive shrimp. Dad had a big-

ass thick lock. He put on the back doors. He then made his exit back to New Jersey. Now picture this scenery like I told earlier. Every other block was a red light, which was long. You were jumping up and down on the cobblestone road, and you have been up since 2:00 a.m. Well, all right. At one of these lights, one of Fulton's famous groups pulled up behind him, cut the lock, and stole the shrimp. How he didn't know I can't even understand. I will tell you these guys are fast and good. Later on in my career, when I was in business, I personally witnessed this happening in broad daylight in the middle of South Street when the traffic was backed up. Well, he got back to the store and told Atlas Foods the story. He asked them if they had more shrimp. The reply was not that was it till one or two months for the new shipment to arrive. He couldn't wait. He needed the shrimp or he would've lost his major customer. He was in sheer desperation. His friends at Atlas Foods met up with some of the big guys in the market and explained what happened. Well, like they say everything can be resolved. It was. Dad had to buy back his own shrimp. Unbelievable—there was no other choice.

Another Shore House Memory

This memory could have ended in a very tragic situation. This was with my brother Jimmy. He was very young and ran away across the street. Luckily, the neighbor saw him jump in the lagoon. She ran after him and then jumped in and saved his life—his lucky day. Well, not all good things can last forever. The property was surrounded by undeveloped land, which was always moist and would produce these gigantic green head flies. When they would bite you, your arms would swell up. So with this being said, Dad built a new house with a swimming pool. He decided to sell the house.

Background of My Extracurricular Childhood Activities

Mom wanted the very best for us; she wanted us not to miss out on anything. She wanted to provide us with every opportunity out there. That summer in camp, we rode on ponies. I took such a liking to horseback riding she enrolled me in horseback riding lessons. I actually did very well and won a couple of ribbons in the shows I participated in. I actually want to take it to the next level as a jockey. But that didn't work too well. First thing, the flies would not let up; they would always be attacking the horses and the rider. Then the smell—there was horse shit all over the place, and in the warmer times, it was disgusting. Then the biggest and most important was my weight. I was a growing boy, and that's something nature can't stop. I did move on to guitar lessons privately. It was fun, a lot of work and practice. At that time, we were learning with the Beatles songs.

Still to this day, I remember playing and singing the songs "Hey Jude" and "Yellow Submarine."

The next adventure was ice skating. There was a local ice rink in town, which we would go to all the time for lessons and practice. They would have general skating sessions on Friday nights. A lot of the kids from different parts of the town would hang out there. They would have loud music playing, and it was a lot of fun. We would race around, showing off to the nice-looking girls how well we could skate and go fast for their attention.

The next adventure from ice skating, we began—we being myself and my brother—to play ice hockey. Ice hockey, if you are not familiar with it, is a very physical sport, an expensive sport. This sport was an early-morning activity. Most ice rings were booked to capacity. The only time allowed for ice hockey would be early mornings. This was not a major problem since we came from a fish family who started the day out in the wee hours of the morning. My mom, I remember, would drive my brother two hours away at 4:00 a.m. for practice. This sport was very demanding for the parents and my brother and me. You really had to be in good shape and be prepared to bang and get banged around.

Beginning of Work Career

My Saturday work program consisted of washing the trucks inside and out and clean the garbage area. I also wiped down the counters and showcases and scales. I would stock the shelves with different grocery items. I would fill up the bags and containers. I did many different chores. I had a full day, for a young boy. As I grew older, so did my responsibilities. I started getting more into the business. I was now filling up the showcases with ice and fish. I was very observant; this business mesmerized me. When I was younger, I would always like to poke and touch the dead fish and play with their eyes. It would amuse me. The smell and stink and blood was cool. I enjoyed going to work. I remember getting a starting pay of $5 to $10 a day. My savings grew and grew, and so did my ambitions. I also had a paper route during the week. The entrepreneur in me started coming out in full force. As I got older, I would go snow shoveling with my friends. I also started cutting some lawns. I was making money all over the place. As time went on, my brother grew older, and he saw what I was doing and wanted to get into the mix. So now I was working every other Saturday, sharing with my brother. I was the favorite choice to work because I had my heart and soul in the job. He was just in it for the money. I was okay with the sharing of Saturdays. I joined a bowling team on Saturday afternoons. I learned a lot from my Saturday job.

Actually, my two first cousins were working full-time for Dad. One cousin, Rudy, was a very good mentor for me. In those hours I spent with him on Saturday, he taught me many good things in this journey of life. He taught me manners, cleanliness, to be courteous to people, how to cook, and most of all, organization. He was a very meticulous person and courteous. This is why he was so successful with his own business and his personal life with his wife and children. My other cousin, Bob, was actually the opposite. Don't get me wrong—he was a good person. But everything turned against him. He had nothing but problems with his wife and horrifying children. To sum it up, he died at a very young age. His wife was screwing his best friend. Like they say, what are friends for?

This is the story of my two cousins. They both were from Brooklyn, New York. My dad promised them a good job and career and future. As years went on, they both learned the business, and it was running perfectly. Dad started taking family vacations. Time went on, and it was time to take the business to the next level—either grow the business bigger and get incentives and large bonuses or some form of partnership for my cousins. Well, Dad fucked up. He chose the words *greed* and *laziness*, and he did nothing for them. This left my cousins with no choice but to move on with their careers.

One day, an opportunity opened up for a retail fish market for sale. The owner, Joe, was retiring. My cousins knew of the store. They swept it right up, seagull diving for fish carcasses. The business was a little rundown, but that was not an issue for Cousin Rudy. He took over that store, renovated it, and brought his personality and gift of gab, and boy, did that business grow. Dad had to recruit a new team. Vacations were now limited, and trustworthy good employees were few and far between. Mom started working in the store again. My brother and I were now older and could take care of customers and take on more responsibility. Our cousin Steve even worked the store on Saturdays and holidays and summers. Dad was very secretive about certain things. He actually would not teach me how to cut—I mean filet—a fish. With my observation of constant staring at him cutting fish, I would actually practice on fish when he was not present. God's honest truth, that's how I learned. It took determination and practice, but I did. It was the same for opening clams and oysters. My brother and I both learned. This was a big bonus for us to master shellfish opening. We would contract some opening shellfish gigs and some from the country club when they had special events. They would contract us for—I don't remember exactly—but it was like $40–$60 a bushel to open the shellfish. In those days, we were in seventh heaven with that money. When I saw you can actually make that kind of money part-time, I started a catering/clambake business. I would get customers from the retail store or advertisements in the local paper. We would either open clams and oysters or I would come with a crew of waitresses and prepare clambakes in people's backyards, start to finish. You want to talk about money—it was fantastic.

Dad's First Step to Modernization

He had a large lobster tank installed in the front window of the store. Wow, this was a traffic stopper. People would stop their cars, get out, and look at the lobsters swimming. He also had rows of tanks in the basement, which could hold thousands of pounds of these crustaceans. Dad would usually receive a call on Saturday afternoon from Point Pleasant Coop. They would let him know that there was an offshore boat coming in with lobsters and fish. Oh no, my day would now end at 11:00 p.m. This journey began at 5:45 p.m. once the store was closed and iced up. Dad and I hurried on to the Garden State parkway to Exit 98. We reached the coop and met a very simple man with a naval-style crewcut named Harry. He was the manager of the coop. We also saw some of the regulars, some of Dad's market buddies, such as John Wooley. Harry dispatched the lobster crates and cartons of fish to us. Dad and I loaded up and were on our way. It would now be roughly 7:30 p.m.

What was next? It was so predictable—dinnertime at the OB Diner. We requested a window seat to make sure our load of seafood would still be there when we finished dinner. Well,

off to Upper Montclair. We arrived, and Dad and I unloaded these massive crates down the stairs and into the tanks. We didn't know what surprises were in these crates. It being an offshore boat, we were deemed to get a lot of jumbo lobsters. By jumbo, I mean we pulled a twenty-five-pound lobster out one night. Some of these lobsters were weak; they didn't survive. Well, here we went—cooked lobsters and lobster meat. The white shoe polish went on the front window (Lobster Special), the neon sign flashing colored lights on the lobster tank. This drew a lot of attention to prospective lobster customers. This looks like a lobster go go bar.

Junior High Years

I was now in junior high. There were many crazy things going on. We would cut school and go up to Essex Green Shopping Plaza and hang out. We would even go as far as taking the bus and subway and going to Aqueduct Race Park in New York. We were very adventurous. I and my friends were very shy at this time around girls. There were some of the sport jocks already dating. On Friday nights,

the couples would meet at the park and have make-out sessions. Sometimes they would be lucky enough to go to someone's house, and they would play spin the bottle. It was okay—we were a little jealous, and we needed to crawl out of our shells.

Choosing college courses was not very easy. We had a big argument that night. My mom was insistent for me to go to college and take all the prep classes. I told her I hated school and wanted to work with fish. My dad was in the middle. He replied, "If you choose the fish business, you will always have a job during good times and bad, meaning war or depression. People have no choice—they have to eat. They don't have to buy clothes or a car, but they must always eat."

In junior high, I played on a lot of different baseball teams and made a lot of lifelong friends that I'm still in contact with today. In the summer, when school was out, I joined the police athletic league baseball team known as PAL. We played all summer long; it was fun. I met a lot of friends and kept busy and out of trouble. That's what these summer leagues were meant for, to keep the kids occupied. When school started, I joined the local baseball league, which would be early evening games. Practice would be on Saturdays. I was on this one team, the Padres, with my friend Neil. We would always be screwing around and making jokes. Well, our regular coach was out sick, so we had a sub who was actually a high school student. He was about four or five years older than us. We were busting on him big time. He overheard and got really mad. He called us down this hill away from everybody and said to us, "Okay, tough guys, bring it on." This grown man twice the size of us tried to beat us up. We both were looking for weapons to defend ourselves. We eventually just ran to safety, back to the field.

I was very close with Neil, and there was another friend, Mark G. We would take bike trips to Verona Pond to go fishing or even further; we would go all the way to Montclair to get hot

Italian subs. Those were the days were we didn't expect much from life, and the littlest things like biking two hours to get a sub sandwich would bring joy to our eyes. Life was easier—no cell phones and computers to destroy our lives. We were always outside, keeping busy and exercising. Nowadays these kids are turning to hell.

Junior High Most Embarrassing Situation

I was trying out for the football team. All my friends and classmates who were cool were doing the same. First, there was training; everyone would get their own equipment and locker. Some of the personal equipment like cups and jockstraps you would purchase. I was the kind of meticulous person who just had to have everything correct and in order. Each day, we would practice after school and play hard. Everyone would take a shower afterward. Of course, my locker was perfectly stocked with powder, deodorant, cologne, and towels all set for the season.

Well, we were getting closer to the beginning of the season. There were too many players to start off with. Some of them quit and couldn't take the enduring practices. Well, there were still too many. Some of us had to go. Well, it is like anything you need to be in with the right people. I was a quiet kid, wasn't Mr. Popular. I didn't have a relationship with the coach. Well, the day came he read off five names of players. I was one of them to be called in to his office for dismissal. All my close friends were in shock. They couldn't believe it. I was facing the window they were looking into. My face was six shades of red from embarrassment. I was ready to break out in tears. Instead, I was able to flip it around into a joke. As they were looking at me, I made my fingers like a scissor, showing that the scissor represented being cut from the team.

Chapter 3

High School Years

Throughout junior high and high school, I had quite a group of friends. Some were closer than others. Some of my close friends were Neil and Kevin. We would do some crazy things. We would go up to the liquor store and that E. J. Korvette shopping center with fake IDs and purchase pints of blackberry brandy or pints of old English beer. We would then drink like fishes and run down to the high school dance and crash it. Unfortunately, the liquid courage did not help; we were still helpless when it came to dating girls. Sometimes, Neil would come by with his older neighbor, Dean, who was seventeen years old and had a VW bug. He would take us driving around looking for girls until one day, we found two girls hitchhiking, and we stopped the car and picked them up. Well, one was a dud, and the other was a little hottie. The dud went home, and the hottie, whose name was Donna D, was in the back with Neil. Well, they became very comfortable together. I was in the front with Dean and we kept looking in the mirrors and saw Neil with his wandering hands all over her. Well, we finally dropped her off, and they exchanged phone numbers. They started meeting each other up at the bowling alley. She brought some friends, but they never matched up to her. She had gigantic breasts and rosy red hot lips. She looked at least our age, fifteen or sixteen years old.

One weekend, Neil had gone away on a family vacation. I had gone up to the bowling alley to hang out, and there was Donna. She asked about Neil, and I told her he was away for two weeks. Her eyes lit up like fireworks. She asked me if I wanted to take a walk outside with her. I did. I didn't know what to expect. She led me into the woods, and there was this large, deep hole, which she knocked me down into. She started grabbing my personal parts and kissing me. Things started getting heated up, and it became crazy for two straight weeks. Wow, this hole was given the famous name of the Pit.

Some other events were at the South Mountain skating arena. On Friday nights, we would skate around like madmen, listening to David Bowie, trying to impress the girls from the other side of town who didn't know us. Yes, it finally worked. I got a bite on my line. Her name was Jane. We sat, talked, and exchanged phone numbers. I called her the next day with Neil next to me. She told me she would like to meet me at Stagg Field next Friday night. Neil looked at me and said, "You know what that means, Holz."

I said, "I know." Well, I didn't expect this. The talk at the rink was if the girl wanted to go to Stagg Field, you definitely gonna get done. Well, it didn't quite end up like that, but it was an adventure. We were all between fifteen and sixteen years old. It was a weird age. We were a little too young to go clubbing, so we needed to make our own fun. One of us had a car, and we would take trips out to Forty-Second Street. There was every-

thing you wanted out there from fake IDs to alcohol, drugs, whorehouses, and peep shows. It was like heaven. Of course there was always a risk, and it was dangerous. There were all kinds of characters, including the hookers; they were the biggest crooks. We would frequent this one place called Show World— it was a peep show place. We would go in there with five or six guys and started getting loud. We were drunk.

One night, this big, black bouncer came up to me and Neil and jumped in our face, screaming, "No peeking. You need to pay." We said okay. Five minutes later, he came back all pissed and said to us, "Do you know what I am going to do now?"

We were shitting in our pants and said, "No, what?"

"I am going to tell you no more peeking." The way he said it was so funny we were dying of laughter.

Another night in sin city, we went out with Black Bart and his GTO all revved up, and of course, Crazy Kevin was with us. Well, of course, everyone was shit-faced, and McHughster, aka Kevin, decided to headlock a hooker as she was trying to rob him. McHughster screamed to Bart to hit it. He jammed on the gas and dragged the hooker fifty feet before letting loose. She deserved it; it was so funny to see this.

Well, senior year—it was Memorial Day. Everyone was in their cars and heading down the shore. The destination was Seaside Heights. Well, it was the beginning of craziness, starting off with the McHughster, one sick dude. As the book goes on, he just becomes sicker and sicker. You will see. I will stop here. Well, it was a feat for him to polish off a six-pack of beer before hitting Exit 135 south on the parkway. The starting point was West Orange, going down Route 280, getting on Exit 145. No one could beat his record. Well, of course we had no motel reservations and nowhere to stay, and all the motels in Seaside Heights were booked to capacity. So we had some friends at the Sea Garden Motel. We went there and were hanging out and drinking. Well, we weren't the only ones with that idea. There were so many people on the balcony. Things were getting crazy. People were so drunk one kid tried to dive off the second floor into the pool. Kids were pissing off the balcony.

Well, there was one very rowdy kid. He was wearing a Mountain High School sweatshirt and was known as Black Bart. Finally, the cops came, and this kid cursed out the cops. They didn't take that too lightly. They announced over the loudspeaker from their police car, "You with the Mountain High shirt, drop your bags. You're going to jail." Then they started pulling kids into the police cars. I and my friends scattered. I actually sweet-talked my way into one of the rooms that some real hot girls from Belleville were renting. I was hanging out with them, acting very innocent. Ha ha. If you knew me, you would know there was a plan. I couldn't decide which one I would bang first. My buddies were getting pissed because I had hit the jackpot. They were trying like hell to weasel into the room. Under no circumstances did these girls want to deal with these drunk, rowdy guys. Well, my friend Neil found his way into the room next door. He decided to crawl through the air-conditioner ducts to our room so he could share the goodies with me. Well, all of a sudden, we heard a loud bang—it was the Neilster. He fell through the ceiling in the bathroom. After that, it didn't end well. We all ended up sleeping in the car at the rest area on the parkway.

Graduation Night

Well, it finally happened. We were getting the hell out of school and officially being tossed into this world. The ceremony was over, which was at the South Mountain Arena, where we had many memories. My uncle Joe was taking pictures of my cousin Nancy, who also graduated with us. He then asked me to join the photos, then Neil was with me, and he addressed him, "Friend, please move over so I can take the picture."

Well, after the photo shoot, Neil and I got the 411 that everyone was going to hang out and celebrate. It was in the parking lot of E. J. Korvette. Well, the cops didn't bother us; it was our night. Everyone was there—there were the nerds, the freaks, the hoodlums, the sport jocks, the ugly, nasty girls, and the parade of hotties. One of the memories of that night that made Neil and myself piss in our pants was Joey Vals—quite a kid, very shy, liked the racetrack. He had a box of *tiparillos*; he was smoking one. We were hanging out getting drunker than drunk, and then some of the top hotties of the class were next to us. Well, out of nowhere, Joey went up to this hotster and had a super serious face. "Hi, Carol. Can I interest you in a *tiparillo*?" We fell to the ground with laughter; you would never expect that.

Beginning of Restaurant Career

I started my restaurant career at a restaurant called the Manor, which is a very famous restaurant in the state of New Jersey. I started working as a clam and oyster opener part-time at sixteen years old. I was such a good employee they started teaching me about the pantry department—salads, dressings, cold soups, etc. I was a natural. They love me especially with the name Holz. I was in like Flint. That restaurant was completely

German-run and controlled; everybody was German. As time passed, opportunities kept opening up. People would quit or get fired or call out sick. They gave me a chance at the vegetable station one day, all types of preparation and cooking of fresh vegetables. Well, it was time to serve the different vegetables a la carte. More opportunities opened. I was promoted to the fish station. This was big time. I worked under the famous Italian chef Michael Abbate. He would not give anyone a chance or teach them. He fought daily with the other chefs and had many a temper tantrum. For the love of God, Mike took me under his wing like I was his son. He was patient and taught me things that you could learn in the best culinary schools in the world. We were very close. I believe that's where my Italian heritage helped. I did get the opportunity to work the broiler station with Jaime. He taught me when he could; he was always sloshed. I did learn from some of my other mentors. I also had the opportunity to work with the head chef, Pasquale, who taught me everything he could. I had the opportunity to learn from the resident butcher every Saturday morning how to break down a leg of veal, trim up filet mignons, and cut shell steaks. I basically had the greatest culinary training hands on and got paid for it. My mentors have left and moved on to open some of their own restaurants, which are some of New Jersey's finest and famous. I worked many hours and went to high school, which I graduated, which was a miracle. My life was the Manor. I didn't care for school. Most of the time I worked seven days. There was always a problem; someone called out. I felt I owed my manager Egon for giving me such opportunities. I never refused him.

My hours were Monday 12:00 p.m. to 11:00 p.m., Tuesday 12:00 p.m. to 11:00 p.m., Wednesday 12:00 p.m. to 11:00 p.m., Thursday 12:00 p.m. to 11:00 p.m., Friday 12:00 p.m. to 11:00 p.m., Saturday 6:00 a.m. till 1:00 a.m., and Sunday

9:00 a.m. to 11:00 p.m. I would earn roughly $500 a week gross and end up with $290 take-home. Unbelievable. While all this guy did was work, he missed out having fun with his friends and girlfriend, right? Well, you are wrong. I had plenty of fun and got paid. How? The Manor is like the Disneyland of restaurants. There are so many different kitchens, dining rooms, offices, laundry, and they even have their own bakery. I was not the only one having fun. It was one big party where you got paid. The waiters and waitresses were either smoking pot, drinking, or having sex in isolated, private areas. Waiters and bartenders were trading liquor to the chefs for all kinds of food for themselves. Most of my high school friends and classmates worked on a buffet station. There were plenty of guys and girls from other towns of high school age that were also there. Then after work, which was basically the same time for everyone, people would meet at different bars and keep on partying. Let me tell you it was a fucking buffet of women at work. I dated more girls there than if I went to a nightclub. They were ready and willing—there were no bullshit games. Everyone was out for a good time. There were plenty of good times and action.

Richie got this fancy powder-blue Camaro for his birthday. One night after work, I was very tired, had a few drinks, and had a fight with my sexy English girlfriend from England, Julia. She was a waitress where I worked at the Manor. Julia was older than me. I was still in high school, and she was in college. She had this light-blue Volks bug; she actually picked me up a few times. It was my first time making love in the back of a Volk—what an experience. Her accent was so sexy it just made me curl. The night was rainy, and

my defroster was not working well. I began to chase her out of the restaurant parking lot. Anyway, I started chasing her down Eagle Rock Avenue until all of a sudden, I was out cold, no vision, just "Rhiana" playing from my Fleetwood Mac eight-track tape. I still say I was dead on arrival and God gave me a second chance. It was in front of the diner. There was a pickup truck parked in the street, and the driver was inside having a coffee. All I know is I claimed the driver pulled out with no signal. How the hell did I come up with that story? My eyes opened. I had driven under the pickup truck roughly 60 mph. I was half under the truck and ended up in the middle of the road with the roof on my shoulders. I freaked out and I got out of the car and ran up the street to a phone booth and called my father. He came and the car got towed to the junkyard. I don't know what else happened. I can't believe I survived and didn't get put in jail

Henns and Holz

Okay, we will call this heading "Henns and Holz" for my friend Neil. He had this old black Chevy he would beat around with. We would grab some liquor, take it up the different wooded trails, and just go crazy driving and knocking trees down. We would have these intense conversations in the middle of the woods and just keep driving as fast as we could until the car would wipe out. This was what we called four-wheeling.

A Field

One day, we were all liquored up, and we went by the high school ballfield and we had a dare contest. It was that I couldn't go around the field and a certain amount of time. Well, I took that dare with my Pontiac, and I floored the car toward the field within fifty feet of the street. The car just sank. It was like we were in quicksand. We all looked at each other. "What the fuck—we are screwed." Here came a cop. Well, I told them to shut up. I got it. In a dead serious, shaken-up voice, I told the cop we had been cut off by some out-of-control kids and it was our only escape route. He bought it hook, line, and sinker. He then called a tow truck for us…what a sucker!

Embarrassing Moment in High School

I was a very big collector of old-time baseball cards. So were my close friends and some classmates. We would send away for different cards. We would attend many card conventions. We would trade with each other or even strangers at conventions. At this time in our lives, we would live and die for this hobby. This actually started in junior high and finished in high school. We would run home from school to see if the mailman had brought our card delivery. We would have the delivery calculated to the hour when they would arrive.

Well, one day, one of the classmates had a collection that you couldn't believe. It had Babe Ruth and Lou Gehrig in Goudey cards. This was irreplaceable. This kid brought them in to school to show one of his buddies. So what happened was the word spread, and now six people saw the cards. Well, the long and short of it was the cards were in his locker when he went to class. When he came out, it was like magic—they were gone, vanished, no more. This kid didn't know what to do. He contacted the principal. They then thought they would replay what happened. All the people that saw the cards were called out of class in the middle of the day. Each person was inter-rogated separately. We were each accused of stealing the cards.

This was quite embarrassing. He wanted us to turn someone in or give them ideas who might have done it. None of us would give any information. We all didn't have any knowledge how they disappeared. Well, it was quite a mystery how this happened and how the person that took the cards didn't get caught. It wasn't complex thinking how this was done. It was easy to solve. I guess then there were more idiots than now. Well, after many years have gone by, one night, under sworn circumstances in our confessional box, the truth came out. I can't divulge who and how to protect all parties.

By the way, the term *confessional box* is used quite a few times in the book. If you forgot from earlier, it is a specific time when a group of only our very close friends are together. We are so, so lit up on booze and drugs and just so high we just confess to each other our sacred secrets and crazy embarrassments we kept from each other.

Chapter 4

I had graduated high school, and that September, I was starting school at the Culinary Institute of New Hyde Park. September came, and I made it up to the institute. It lasted two weeks. It was basically insulting my intelligence. I was so far advanced I didn't have the patience for jibber jabber. They were teaching students to crawl, and I was already in the Olympic track meet. Also another important dealbreaker was I was surrounded by all guys except for a couple of dyke girls. I ventured outside the campus and discovered an all-girls college, which was very far away. This situation was not going to work for me. I was a young stud in heat. I ended up leaving the culinary school and ended up back in New Jersey. I started working for Dad again and part-time at night as a chef. There I was once again decorating the front window with the white shoe polish advertising some specials. In the morning, our competitor, Valley Seafood, an older couple, Lenny and his wife, would make a slow drive and stare at that window; they saw the reckoning of their business in front of them. I would receive my daily dirty look as the prices went up. They were an easy target. They decided to sell out and take cover. The new owner didn't have a fighting chance. He was an ex-employee of our other competitor, Montclair Seafood. He worked as a buyer and on the wholesale end of the business. His retail experience was limited. He was also a little rough. These stores needed TLC and also great fish and a good bullshitter to sell the fish. Well, like I predicted, it wasn't long till that store closed up for good. Not bad, Richie—one down, one to go.

Well, the next one wouldn't be that simple. His main business was wholesale seafood distribution. I had a sense of jealousy over his company. I would always see these fish trucks brightly colored all over making deliveries to all the local restaurants. At a young age, even I could see dollar signs all over. I counted at least seven trucks parked in back of their store. We only had two trucks, and we were living pretty well. I could only imagine four times that. The cash register would keep ringing—*cajing, cajing*. On the trucks were lettered "We cater clambakes." This brought more thoughts into my head.

Well, as time went on, Montclair Seafood opened an extension in Livingston inside a local supermarket. He then went on to open a seafood restaurant next to his store in Montclair. To me, something was wrong with this picture. This guy was full speed ahead with his boat, and my dad was still parked at the dock. It seemed like he had a license to print money. I would, day after day, badger my father to get off his ass and let us move ahead. It seemed like he didn't want to interfere with this guy's customers. Back in the day, there was common courtesy, and everyone more or less stayed in their own backyards. They didn't go around stealing other people's accounts on purpose. They would work through recommendation, or if their chef switched restaurants, they would follow. Well, I thought differently; this was the new generation. I promised my dad someday I would have a business bigger than Montclair Seafood, and he would be out of business. Well, my promise came true. Unfortunately, Dad passed away before he could see that.

Now Montclair Seafood went bankrupt, and the property was bought by Dunkin Donuts, and now this monumental seafood company was serving coffee and donuts. It was a new error starting. Times were changing and sanitation practices were being enforced—temperature control, etc. I had many talks with Dad. "Change is good. You must go with the flow or you will be left behind, Dad." The business was not going anywhere fast. His competitor Montclair Seafood just redid his store. The other competitor, Valley Seafood, just changed ownership with some new ideas and changes to that store. So he finally agreed to have a gentleman named Andy from Eggert Refrigeration Company come down and design an updated, modern-day seafood center. He did just that. This store was the kick-ass retail seafood store of Montclair. We had a salad case with all home-made goodies that I prepared, a stand-up freezer case with all heat that served seafood specialties that I also prepared, and a shellfish case with all types. We had a ten-foot fish case with every kind of filet and fish you can imagine.

Well, after six months, sales had doubled. Dad was in astonishment. He kicked himself in the ass for not doing this sooner. Our first Christmas with the new setup was bizarre. We were both in shock. We sold every kind of fish we had. There were lines wrapped around the block just to get into the store. It was a very merry Christmas for dad. The success of this makeover was incredible. My experience working in some of the top restaurants made me create some creative food. My own seafood salad was known as the casino salad. The salads became so popular we were approached by a local gourmet deli if we could make these salads for their establishment. Well, we did. It became so busy we couldn't keep up with all the work. The deli owner and Dad, who had a hot temper, got into it. Dad told him off, and he told him, "Have a good life. See you in Naples, Artie," whatever that meant.

"Oh, that lobster tank in the window." You know that song, "Oh, look at the doggie in the window"? Well, my dad, Artie was so proud he would say, "Oh, look at those lobsters in the window." He was quite a different guy. You would never expect some of the things that would come out of him. He was a tough, angry man. He did have a humorous side if you were lucky enough to catch it. He treated some of his fish and shellfish with more love than his kids. I will give you some examples. His famous lobsters were housed up and downstairs. He would cut pieces of hand-cut market cod strips and actually feed them each day. The softshell crabs were live. He would handle them like they were newborn

infants. He would tuck the softies and his clams in at night with brown cloth potato bags. This was so they wouldn't catch a cold. He was such a caring dad for his product.

Okay, getting back to the lobster tank in the window. I must include cousin Steve, aka the King's Highway Seafood Master. The funniest would be the electric light switch on the side of the lobster tank with an open outlet. There were some kids that would put their hands in the lobster tank and splash the water on the floor. Steve and I would have to clean it up. There was this one kid that would always come in with his mom and would never listen to her. He never, never learn his lesson. By not learning his lesson his ritual would be entering the store walk toward the lobster tank. When Mom was ordering her fish, he would then proceed to splash the water out of the tank. His hands were wet. Then he would proceed to the light switch. With his dripping wet hands, he would try to turn the fish market in to a disco. Moving the lights on and off, after a couple of times of playing with the switch, he dripped water on the switch, and he got shocked. You never saw a kid jump so fast. He didn't know what hit him. Steve and I saw the whole thing. We busted up in tears laughing so hard. We had to leave the store.

Another story would be taking the lobsters out of the tank and weighting them in the bag. We were so proud of ourselves selling water for lobster prices. Steve and I knew it was just the beginning. Steve and I enjoyed eating lobster roe and their eggs. Most people didn't know what it was, or some thought it was disgusting. We would offer the customers if they would like their lobsters cooked and split. If they said yes, we would ask them if they wanted the roe and eggs removed. If they said yes, there would be joy in our eyes. We would have our little private feast in the back room. I invented the saying of this feastly dish Pate de Langoste. Sometimes I would spread it on Ritz crackers. What a feast!

Another Cousin Steve story—this involves my brother Jimmy and Steve. I was actually not involved in the actual disaster. I just orchestrated it. One weekend, my dad received a bunch of live lobsters at a great price. That meant my brother, Steve, and Dad were expecting great sales that weekend. I was just helping out, cooking a few things. That Saturday morning on the way to work, Steve and my brother stopped at Pathmark to pick up a few things early in the morning. They spotted signs all over about a special they had on live lobsters. The price was a lot cheaper than our price. That meant war. What to do? Well, there was only one thing to do: attack the enemy. The two fish soldiers proceeded to the beverage section. They were told to grab two packages each of red punch juice and pink lemonade and proceed to the lobster tank. They then opened up the packages and poured them into the tank. Lo and behold, the problem was solved. The tank was filled with red and pink water with a heavy concentrate of citric acid. Well, all the lobsters died, the tank had to be emptied, and we had great lobster sales.

Well, getting back to Cousin Steve—his mom died when he was about seventeen years old. He became very close to my dad and the rest of our family. I believe Dad felt like what his sister Ellen, Steve's mom, did for him, he should do the same for her son. Well, he blended in with us, and we all got along. He was like a second brother to me and Jimmy. Mom and Dad both welcomed him with open arms. He was very close to his father and sister when they were all together

My cousin Robin was getting married. This was being held in a very Jewish catering hall. I was there with my girlfriend. We were drinking, and I was getting looped. We began to fight at the wedding reception, so I was told to get up from the table. I began to walk around the wedding hall. I spotted this little hottie in the coat check room. I stopped and started my sweet talk. It didn't take very long. I smuggled her a couple of drinks to loosen her up more. Before you knew it, we were in one of the back rooms making out and more. Well, the party was ending; she had to give out the coats. So we exchanged phone numbers.

Well, that wasn't the end; actually, that was the beginning of some more history. I started going out to the Queens to see her. This was a trip. Like I said, I always thought of my good friend Neil. I asked her if she had a friend. She did, so we hooked them up together. So now I had my partner in crime with me to take this journey back and forth. We were on a hot streak. We would meet up with them during the week on a couple of off nights. We would go out there, do our business, and head back to Jersey. One of our favorite spots, which I named Muldoon's Point, was a secluded area by a waterfront where people would park and do their business. This name came from the famous show *Happy Days*, where Fonse would go with his babes. It was so crazy; the girls would ask, "Where are we going?"

There was a mumble coming out from the back from the Hens, aka Neil chanting, "Muldoons, Muldoons."

Well, there always is an ending to every good moment. One night on the way back to Jersey, I was driving and closed my eyes for a second. Now remember at this point I had my own business and was going down to Fulton Street every day at 4:00 a.m. and partying all night till all hours. I did not have proper rest. We bounced off the guard rail. That was our wakeup call. This is when the GUD came into effect—geographically undesirable. We decided our lives weren't worth a piece of ass, so the story ended.

Something happened when my cousin Steven broke loose from them and the relationship dwindled between them. For some reason, the relationship with his father and sister also caused friction with our family. They wanted nothing to do with us either.

Well, one day, one of the steady retail customers called, and she was a little snippy with me on the phone. I don't remember exactly what happened, but I answered her back—not nasty or rude but just put her in line. Well, it was one of those situations that was hearsay. Who do you believe? It really wasn't a big deal. So my dad screamed and embarrassed me in the store. I couldn't believe he turned on me and chose the customer over me. I had put my blood and soul in his store to make it right. This was my payback. I lost it. I broke out in tears and went on a rampage. I told him I fucking quit. I left abruptly.

My dreams were in front of me. I needed to learn the wholesale seafood business. So I started thinking, *Learn from the biggest and one of the best wheelers and dealers.* The next morning, I took a trip to downtown Brooklyn. My god, I thought I would never get there. I finally found it, but there were no parking spots. I had no idea what I was bargaining for. I was the only white thing on the street. Well, I found it: M. Slavin and Sons. It was like a little city—trucks all over the place. tons of fish all over. They had a retail market with ten people working in it. There was fish being loaded into the basement. Well, I made it to the office and told my story. Then someone brought me downstairs to another office. Inside was a big, burly man named Barry. He was one of the brothers. His son came into the office later on to join in. Well, Barry questioned me and drilled me like I was a spy. I was very truthful and told him my history and experience. He offered me a position with a low starting salary. I told him I would get back to him. I had a lot of thinking to do. The transport back and forth would be very challenging. Well, I didn't take it. My mom put my dad and I back together again.

I was now around nineteen and working full-time in Dad's store. I would do some part-time at one of the restaurants. I did not give that up. I had a passion for cooking and creating. I would go out almost every night of the week clubbing. Each club had their special night when it was so crowded and everyone would go. A lot of the same people would follow the system. In the summer months, the guys would all chip in and rent a shore house. Depending on what we could find, it would be either Belmar or Seaside Heights. My friends would start their journey down the shore Friday afternoon and either come back home Sunday night or Monday morning. I of course was on a different schedule. I always had a job or responsibility. I would come down on a late Saturday afternoon and leave late Sunday night. I can dedicate a book alone to these weekend shore trips. The events that took place are close to being unbelievable. If you heard or saw the TV series *Jersey Shore*, that was nothing. Most of the things that happened were so crazy and illegal. We, meaning the crew, would all be in jail if this took place currently.

Okay, here are a couple of quick stories. Belmar, one year, we were in one of the houses with maybe ten different people that rented this four-bedroom house with all different personalities staying there. There were wild, crazed guys to well-groomed college kids. Well, it was late afternoon. There was myself, Black Bart, Neil, and a beautiful girl named Jenny. Jenny was taking a shower, getting ready for her date. Well, the doorbell rang. I answered the door and asked this regular-looking guy who he was looking for. He then proceeded to say Jenny. I asked him his name. He said, "Bruce Springsteen." I was drinking and was well-buzzed. I thought this guy was busting my balls. We didn't think anything of it because she was drop-dead gorgeous. I screamed up to Neil to tell Jenny Bruce Springsteen was here for his date. Meanwhile, I thought, *This guy is fucking with me.* I offered him a beer and to sit down. Neil proceeded to come down to see who this guy was. He was so curious to see what this guy looked like to land beautiful Jenny. Neil was more into rock than I was. I was more of a disco duck. We would dream to have her as a girlfriend.

Neil saw him and almost shit in his pants. He screamed out loud, "Holy shit, Holz, it's fuckin' Bruce!" Well, that was it. Neil wouldn't let him leave. He had to get pictures with him. Then Jenny came down and grabbed Bruce and left for their date. Jenny really didn't think it was a big deal to date Bruce Springsteen. He was just playing local gigs, and his fame was there but not like currently. To this day, we believe the song "Jenny Jenny" was created for our summer house friend Jenny.

Another episode: Black Bart was misbehaving and would get really sloppy drunk. We did not want him to go out with us because he was like a scarecrow. He would chase the girls from us in the clubs with his poor appearance and dirty mouth. Well, Kevin had an idea. I had police handcuffs. So a couple of us carried him to this tree in the front of the house. We then proceeded to handcuff him to the tree. He was actually passed out from drinking. When he woke up, he was a raging bull trying to break loose. He couldn't. He was screaming, then the cops came and freed him from the handcuffs.

Here is the next story. We were plastered on beer with open and closed beer in the back seat. We were then stopped by the Lavalette police driving up a one-way street the wrong way. We were such bullshit artists we talked our way out of it.

Another story was down in Seaside. The nightclubs were so crazy busy. Everyone from all over would find their way to the clubs. The lines to get in were wrapped around the block. Instead of us getting out early to wait in line, as we called it, we would "prime up." In simple terms, we would get totally plastered for two reasons: first, so we didn't have to spend a fortune in the clubs, and second, to give us that liquid courage. So when we got inside, we were ready to work again. "Ready to work" meant dancing with some hottie and hopefully bringing her home (and not to meet Mom). Well, you are wondering how we finally got into the clubs without waiting in lines. There was one of the crew members; his name was Kevin McHugh (also known as Daddy). This guy was built like a brick shit house. He had straight, light-brown hair, crooked teeth, and had a limited wardrobe. It was very predictable, the clothing he would wear. In the colder months, we called it the bachelor outfit. That consisted of worn-out jeans, which at this time in history was not the style, a flannel shirt, and a corduroy jacket. His footwear was a deep, long pair of boots where he could smuggle into the bars cans of beer. Getting off the subject, one night, we all went out to the Turtlebrook Inn nightclub. Kevin smuggled in about four cans of beer. It just so happened the Turtlebrook doesn't sell that brand. It so happened there was a very observant bouncer that noticed the beer. Kevin was approached and questioned where he got that brand from. Unbelievably, this worm got away with it. He convinced the bouncer they had just started dealing with that brand tonight. This is the kind of stuff that I lived through. Nothing was impossible. He was crazy and had two sets of balls. Getting back down to the shore, he would find the back entrance and walk in, and the bouncers would stop us. He then threw a couple of names out from up of some of the clubs in North Jersey. They would look at him with amazement, and he would just make his way in with us, tagging along. We'd just save a good two hours in line and free admission. This guy was so crazy and very cheap. Well, I really didn't want to write about the club days, but anyone who reads this book who grew up in the eighties will appreciate this. I just don't know where to start. There are so many stories. I will just try to highlight some of the best.

Another funny club story was one Friday night after a big Italian fish dinner. There was all kinds of great food, an unbelievable cook my mother was. This is why my father was never in good shape. I couldn't move after stuffing my face. Besides not able to move after dinner, being exhausted from getting up early to buy dead fish, this combo would knock me out. I would actually pass out until the guys rang the doorbell and come barging into my bedroom with all kinds of goodies and bags of liquor. We then would start to get primed up for a crazy night. Well yes, that night was crazy. We were headed down to Belleville to Parillos nightclub. Of course, we had a late start, and there would be lines to get in, no parking, etc. My stomach was growling the entire trip down from all that good food mixed with all kinds of hard liquor. We arrived, and I started farting like crazy. The guys were getting pissed off with the stink. Then it hit me—I got a sudden attack with no bathroom in sight. Yes, it happened—I shit myself. Basic translation, I shit in my pants. The guys would not take me home especially viewing a waiting line full of hotties. Well, I did not have any choice but one to resolve this nasty problem. I went behind someone's garage and took my underpants off and cleaned up. I then disposed of the goods. That night, I was in the club bare-assed with no underpants. The guys were busting my balls all night. They even told this beautiful girl I met what happened. To this day, I am still reminded of this.

Here is another Parillo story. Neil and I drove down again to the club well-primed on hard liquor. We then proceeded to park outside the club. We were smoking the green, windows up, and really getting fucked up. It was like a scene in a Cheech and Chong movie. Well, I began to tell Neil, "We have to stop and get out of here."

He said, "Fuck that. What are you afraid of, pussy?"

Well, five minutes went by, and a cop pulled up. I spotted him in the mirror and told Neil. He dashed the rest of the green in his jacket liner. We put the fan on high and opened all the windows. Well, the cops pulled up and question us, "What are you guys doing here?"

We said, "We are about to go in to the club." They asked us if we were drinking or if we had any drugs. We said no.

The cop gave Neil another chance. "Are you sure?"

Neil replied, "Nothing."

The cops got so pissed off they grabbed us both and slammed us hard against the car. They searched the car and came up empty handed. Then they searched us. I had nothing. Then he is felt up Neil and found the green. He took it out of his jacket, shoved it in Neil's face, and said to him in a loud voice, "Nothing. You have nothing." He then went into the police car with our licenses. We heard them calling our information into headquarters. They referred to Neil as Foxtrot because of his initials. We were cracking up then caught ourselves. Well, to this day, I still call him Foxtrot. We were both shitting fucking bricks not because we are going to jail but because both our fathers would kick the living shit out of us. The cops came out of the car, handed us our licenses back, and told us, "You guys are very fuckin' lucky. Both of you get the fuck out of my town and never come back. The next time, you won't be so lucky."

Well, we bolted the fuck out of there and said our prayers to God. Did that stop the dynamic duo? No, three weeks later, we returned with a different car and haircuts. Well, it was Wednesday night—that was Joey Harrison's surf club in Fairfield, which was a given. My friends Neil, Kevin, and I were headed to our destination already primed with preclubbing medicine (booze and drugs) and decked out. We were already buzzing. Well, there you go—the liquid courage set in. We were hanging out dancing with the chicks, trying our best to pick one up to leave with. If they refused, at least we tried to get their phone number for a real date. Well, last call—of course we were leaving alone that night. Mechanic McHugh (Kevin) spotted three girls having car problems. Their car wouldn't start. He proceeded over there and said, "Hey, girls, you need some help? I am a mechanic. Let me take a look.' He looked under the hood, and he was looking back and forth. He then proceeded to tell them his diagnosis. Well, in real life, he couldn't put air in a car tire. "Well, girls, it seems to be your wankel nut and fortis valve." He said this with a straight face. Neil and I were bursting out laughing. This numbskull couldn't fix a toy car. Well, we drove them to the diner and hung out—that was it.

Back to Dad's Fish Store

In this little community shopping area, there was an old-fashioned Italian barbershop next door, a shoe repairman, and a tailor. We were all friendly. The barbershop had a hired a cute lady to cut hair; her name was Donna. She was your typical guidette from the North Newark, Bloomfield area. I suddenly got the hots for her, and she started to flirt with me. I would build her up and get her happy. She was older than me, and I was younger. She made her way to the fish store several times when Dad was not present during the day. We actually made out in the back room one day. One afternoon, we were caught in the fish cooler making out by my cousin Steve. One afternoon, Angelo from the shoe repair, Donna the stylist, and I made arrangements to go out after work for dinner. Angelo's girlfriend was going to join us. We had a wonderful dinner and some cocktails to get the party started. Angelo and his girlfriend left, and it was me and Donna. I asked her what she wanted to do; she said, "Have some more fun." We started making out in the car. We had to stop; we were getting crazy. I drove to a local motel and checked in. Wow, what a fucken night. It never ended; she was in heaven. I believe I was only eighteen. Can you imagine the stamina? I discovered she was at least thirty.

We enjoyed each other, but as usual, there was hell to pay. I never came home; she never came home. She was living with some Spanish guy, and I don't know what the relationship was. He could be a roommate, a friend—who knows? Who cares? All I knew was he got hold of my home phone number and was calling my mother and father every half-hour. They told him they didn't know where Donna was. My parents were not worried about me. My dad knew my story; I was a registered whore master. "Not to worry about him," he told my mom.

That Friday morning, I came straight to work after dropping her off at the barbershop. My mother came out with a broom in her hands, and my cousin Steve was signaling me to run before I get hit. I ran from her broom, and she was so mad she hit Steven with it, thinking he knew all along where I was.

Dad's business was fantastic; he was now getting crazier. The devilish word was back—*greed*. He was starting to take interest in the ponies horse racing at the track. He was starting to gamble. On Mondays, he would take a trip to Monmouth racetrack, and on Saturday night, he would go to the Meadowlands. I and my friend Neil would go with him sometimes. He would get caught up with the so-called systems for winning horse racing. He would buy the racing form and the daily post and play with the systems. He realized it was not working. Now he never followed sports before. He now had taken an interest in sports gambling.

There was one of his employees, also a friend, Charlie A, also known as Fat Charlie. Charlie was a stocky, semi-cross-eyed fellow. He knew the laws of the land. He knew when to speak, what to say, and how to present himself. Charlie introduced him to the local bookie, Carmine. He was low-key working out of a gas station as a front. Carmine was a medium-built Italian fellow from north Newark originally. He always had purple-tinted glasses on. It seemed like he even slept with them on. He was not your average gavone. He was a very well-spoken guy. Carmine took a liking to Dad. Actually, his son Mike was working part-time in the fish store, and when Mike was not available, he would have some of his friends fill in. Also one summer, Carmine invited me to go down to their shore house for a week and hang out with his other son, who was my age. Dad started frequently hanging out at the gas station, where he met other guys with the same habits, such as Bob the fireman and Richie "Farfunkle." This nickname that he invented was from a customer who was dressed with a suit and tie and a trench coat and would come into the store with his eighty-year-old mother, and hence, he named them the Farfunkle family. Dad was going up and down with this gambling more down than up. Carmine cut him off; he didn't want it to end badly. Dad moved on to the Passaic crowd. He got involved with some tough guys. He ran into some big problems. These guys would come in on Monday looking for payment. They would go downstairs into the basement, and I would try to listen by the steps what was going on. There was a lot of screaming and cursing. There were some times it sounded like they gave Dad a beating. When he really fucked up, the big cheese came down, Frank S. Dad was addicted; it was worse than drugs. He bet on it all—baseball, football, baskets. Frank also took a liking to

Dad. I believe Frankie cut him off also. He then was at the end of the rope; he had nowhere to play. He had to deal with the hoodlums in the Fulton fish market. Oldman Johnny from peck slip took his action. 

Sometimes it got so bad he sent me down there to buy the fish. Dad lost all his savings and cashed in all the insurance policies. What a mess. Even had this guy Richie's wife on the payroll to pay his debt. My mother saw checks written out to this lady, and she freaked out. He lost interest in the business. He was concerned in gambling, to get his money back. We all know where that theory goes. Your first loss is your best loss. Dad had so much pressure and tension between trying to keep his business intact, supporting his family, and not losing the house and the store.

One Wednesday night, I went out to the surf club in Fairfield, which was a discotheque, with one of my friends. I ordered a drink, and when I grabbed it, I accidentally spilled some of it on this girl. She cursed me out and said, "Watch it, asshole."

I looked at her in the eyes, and she looked in mine, and I ask her, "Do you really mean that?" I said I was very sorry, and she replied, "No, I am sorry also." We began to talk, and it was electric. I fell in love in minutes. She was so beautiful and had such a rack on her. I was in heaven. Her friend was nudging her to leave. I knew I couldn't wussy out now. I asked her for her phone number, and she gave it to me. I believe she had just finished a heavy relationship. I had met her just at the right time. She lived in Wayne. I lived in West Orange. She was very easygoing. We would meet sometimes halfway, or she would just come over my house. We got along like a perfect couple; she had a lot of things in common with me. Since we both came from Italian heritage, we couldn't get enough of each other. Her mom was starting to get sick, and that gave Marianne more responsibility. Then it came that MS had attacked her mom, and she was bedridden forever. Her grandmother also lived with her and her sister and brother. Mom was divorced. We did everything together—vacations, parties, you name it. My love grew for this lady, I became crazed over her. I was so jealous and protective. I even went as far as taking her phone away so no one could call her. One night, I got into a jealous rage at my house and broke her windshield. We separated for a while. I realized I had a problem. I couldn't be without her. I proposed to her and gave her a diamond that would blind your eye. We were officially engaged. Now to set the date. My sister was also engaged. Dad was trying to figure out that one out. How the hell was he going to pay for the wedding? With me, I had no problem. I would take care of my own wedding.

As time went on working for Dad, his business kept growing and so did my ambitions. I wanted to grow the wholesale end of the business. I started to get itchy. I had a talk with Dad and told him I would need his cooperation, giving me prices and information so I could call on new accounts. I called on some of the places I worked. Then I started on others. I was running into a brick wall. I was told by the restaurants my prices were too expensive. I did some investigation. The restaurants were correct. My dad was giving me high prices on purpose. He basically told me he didn't want the business to get bigger. Then I questioned him about my future. How would I get ahead? Would he be willing to give me some partnership? How could I get some real money? Well, I got an answer that he wasn't ready for any changes like that. He replied, "I still have your brother and sisters to take care of. When I retire the business will be yours." Well, my wheels turned, and it didn't have to take to many turns to figure that out. It was time to take my future in my own hands.

Chapter 5A

Well, I did. It started with purchasing my own van. I was going to start my own business and still help out my dad. I used a small portion of his cooler and used his facility to prepare my fish. It was not easy to start from zero at the age of nineteen. This kid had to convince prospective customers that I knew what I was doing and would show up with very fresh product on time and priced fairly. This kid had to be very patient and lose money in the beginning and make a very small salary until the business grew. I kept my head always up and didn't give up. As the business grew, I had to establish credit. I had to convince the different companies in the Fulton fish market I was reputable and would always pay them on time. I will say it did help that they had a relationship with Dad. Well, time went by, and one day, Dad freaked out again. It was the second time for me. He went into the cooler which I was sharing and he couldn't find something. He then proceeded to take all my fish out of the cooler and hurl them like a soccer ball into the parking lot. There were sea scallops on the pavement, which now became breaded with asphalt.

There were a crate of live lobsters, which now became crushed lobster and so forth. He then shouted to me, *"Get the fuck out of my store, and don't come back this time!"* Well, he meant it. I really

couldn't believe the on-the-spot eviction. Well again, it was time to move on with my future and make some major decisions. I had been going to the Fulton market myself and had taken a shortcut home a couple of times.

Chapter 5B

I passed through this busy little town on a very busy main street. It was Ridge Road in Lyndhurst. I then located a storefront. I opened up a retail fried fish and wholesale operation. This was at a very young age. I believe I was twenty years old. Incredible that I did it all by myself. I was able to furnish it with equipment and get all the proper licenses and permits. Off I went. I hired employees, and the business was rocking. Things were going great. During one of one of my quarrels with Merianne, I met a beautiful hottie from north Newark on a Sunday night coming back from a weekend shore excursion at Creations, a local disco. She basically had a very strong appetite for me. She was engaged to some guy in North Arlington, the next town over from my store. She would go to his house, grab his beautiful white Corvette, and come and see me at the store. This way, she had his car, and  he couldn't follow her. She had her path covered. Well, you want to see an attention grabber? She would pull up in the 'vette in front of the store and get out with a short mini to die for. Everyone in the neighborhood had to stop and stare. She came in to the store, headed directly to me, and stared at me with those bedroom eyes. Then we proceeded to go to the back of the store. You could only imagine the rest. She was a school-teacher. *Wow*, why didn't my teachers look like that?

One night, we were on a date, and she decided she want me to see where she worked. Fine, I figured we would just drive in front of the school, but no. We pulled up to the front door, and she told the security guard she forgot some papers in her classroom. He then let us in. We proceeded to the classroom, went inside, and she locked the door. She told me her fantasy was to make love on top of her desk. Well, she didn't have to twist my arm. I accommodated her without any hesitation. Wow, that was different.

I worked very hard to get that business going. I worked many long hours. One day, I had so much fish to cut. I stayed all night till I passed out on the cutting table, snoring. One friend of mine was working the night shift for his job and passed by the store and saw the lights on. He then stopped and banged on the window till I woke up. That's crazy. Then it was time to go to the Fulton market and start a new day. Those were the high-lights of that store. The nightmare was the smell. I had nothing but complaints from the neighbors and town. To shorten the story, I was brought to court by the city and was evicted from the town. The complaint was valid. The garbage would be put out in front of the store and picked up early morning. In the summer, it would cook out there, and you could smell it from the next town.

Another interesting story was my landlord. She was a divorced lady in her forties. She had a thing for me. She knew I had girlfriends and had no problem with hooking up with women. That didn't stop her. She would always make sexual comments to me. It was rent time. So I had called her to come pick it up. She then told me she couldn't and asked if I could drop it off at her house after work. So I didn't think anything. I arrived and rang the bell. She answered the door in a black lace teddy. I was appalled. I said, "I am sorry. Did I wake you?"

She replied, "No, actually the opposite. I was waiting for you." She led me in by hand to her sofa. We sat down. She said, "You look stressed. Would you like a massage?"

I said, "No, it's okay." She didn't accept *no*; she proceeded anyway. Then things went in different directions. Someone rang the doorbell, and her party ended. She told me I didn't have to pay the rent.

She replied, "Maybe we can do this more often." Wow, this was really off the charts.

Here is another story from the Lyndhurst store. One day, my knee was swollen. I didn't think about it because I didn't remember hitting it or any disruption to it. The next day, it was bigger and had some pain and was limping. My mother insisted on bringing me to the doctor. I refused because I had my business and couldn't leave it. Then my aunt Barbara—God rest her soul—joined forces with my mother and dragged me to the doctor. Well, thank God they did that. The doctor pumped out a pint of poisonous pus from my knee. He then had me rushed to the hospital. If I had not been taken care of that day, I probably would have lost my leg. Well, I was away from the business trying to think how I could escape from the hospital. It was impossible. To shorten the story, this was one of my first experiences of the real world of cruelness, thievery, and not to trust anyone. I had some really good employees working for me. My mom was there trying to oversee, but I guess she was more naive than me. She was flimflammed by a salesman I had that was in a wheelchair. He had married one of my classmates and was from the area I grew up in. The story was I had twenty-five cases of u/15 Bumblebee shrimp from Surinam. They were the Mercedes-Benz of shrimp. This shipment was put aside in the freezer for one of my special customers, Casey's Pub. These shrimp were very hard to obtain. The value of this shipment was like eleven thousand dollars. This salesman, Jerry, knew this. He wrote a phony order for all twenty-five cases to a fictitious name. My key employee, Freddie, told him he couldn't sell them. Richard had them saved for Casey's Pub. Freddie told my mom, and she confronted the salesman. He then told her he had spoken with Richard and that I okayed the sale. She bought it hook, line, and sinker. Home run for that son of a bitch. He disappeared after that heist. I had lawyers and investigators looking for him. He was gone. They finally tracked him in California, and he filed bankruptcy. Many years later, we found out he died. Well, he got his. I was still out of the money.

Chapter 5C

The Move: Store No. 2

Well, I found a warehouse building closer to my house at Orange, New Jersey. At that time, that area of Orange was the valley section. There were a good number of Italians. It started getting darker and darker as time went on. I was still very young and didn't have the money for this. I needed to get a mortgage. Yes, a twenty-year-old getting a mortgage? Well, I did. I was an owner of a warehouse building. We moved operations from Lyndhurst to Orange to this large building. This meant more bills, more responsibility. I had to work double. Well yes, I did. I worked my butt off and still had to carry on my personal life. We had a retail store, which we opened up in the front. I went out on the attack. I started gathering more and more customers. We had something like six trucks. We were delivering all over New Jersey. My father had his business, and I had mine. We then bonded again. He was amazed at my actions and how I carried myself and my responsibilities. I would pick up some items he would be short on. He then would pick them up in the morning and see all the business. I was way ahead of what he could ever believe. I even had a brand-spankin'-new El Dorado Cadillac. He asked me to borrow it several times to go to Atlantic City with my mom. How's that, Dad borrowing his son's car? Wow, that made me feel good. While we are on this subject, through Dad's compulsive gambling habit, I even bailed him out lending him ten thousand dollars. When he passed away, he still owed me the money. My mom wanted me to have good thoughts about him, so she paid me from his insurance money.

Well, I started seeing the real world in front of me. I was going down to Manhattan's Fulton fish market every morning.

I would be in for a new adventure every day. Whose turn was it today to try to screw me? There would be short weights, missing items from the truck, etc. I had to follow the laws of the street. I had to pay for parking in the street, aka "security." I would pick out beautiful fish, then they would switch it for the older ones. It was like show and tell. Well, it was quite a learning experience. There was entertainment at the Fulton fish market every day without fail. Some innocent truck driver from down south would drive through the middle of the market without knowing the rules of how the game is played. By the time he had driven no more than five minutes, his trailer would be broken into and all his seafood stolen. Or there would just be common drivers passing through with their cars, and they would get hostile with the market workers, then the workers would gang up and tip over or destroy the driver's car. Or on a quiet day, Shopping Bag Annie would be walking the market with her carriage of goods she would be selling. She was quite a lady in her day. She would flash her giant breasts to whoever whenever. It was a show in itself. I remember when I was a young boy, I was embarrassed to see such a thing. My favorite part of the morning was having a Fulton market breakfast. Let me tell you, from when I was a little boy going down with Dad, the egg and meat sandwiches were to die for. You couldn't get food like that anywhere. Then as years went by, on Fridays up at the club, they had fried fish sandwiches that were incredible. Then I would get back to the warehouse and deal with the employees stealing, drivers shorting the customers packages and trying to steal payments. Then customers would receive their orders. When it came to payment, it was like magic how they disappeared. Or they would always have a good story not to pay. Good paying customers were hard to find. Well, my trust in people wore away quickly. I became a hard person. I wouldn't trust anyone. I would leave my employees locked in the warehouse working while I went to the market. They still underhanded me. They would be cooking expensive fish for breakfast or eating fresh Maryland jumbo lump crab meat at fifteen dollars a pound while I was at the market.

This story follows me to this day. Lunds Fishery (Dennis) was making a delivery to us early morning, and he was knocking on the garage door. The employees told him they were locked in. He couldn't believe it. He said to me I had a new way to keep them working. They couldn't escape. We both laughed about the craziness back then. Well, years later, I did let up my guard and had a family friend work for me. His name was Joe De, nicknamed "Strunz." I did not lock the employees up anymore in the warehouse. I left Joe there working with the other employees. I felt secure with Joe since he was very close to our family. Well, years later, one of the employees, an older black man John, Hobbs, told me in sheer confidence not to tell Joe. It was a shock for me, and I couldn't believe it until he basically told me exactly how it went down. Joe would be stealing fish every day and packing it away in a large cooler in his van. This really set me up a notch. Who could you trust? This guy would eat out of my plate like a brother.

Well, it wasn't all that bad. Come to think of it, there was some playtime also. I definitely was not all there. I did some of the craziest things imaginable. I was single, young, and free. Well, I would hire the best of the best secretaries to answer the phone, take orders, and assist me in sales. I don't know how this happened each time, but it was crazy. These young, attractive girls would always manage to fool around with me. I will just tell you a couple of good ones. I had a go go girl who would work at night and get paid cash. She took the job with me because she needed to file income tax. The money I paid her was ridiculous compared to her night job. Sometimes she would threaten to quit because I would give her too much work, and she would tell me what to do with my job and fish. Well, I grew on her. She took more than a liking to me. Well, to get to the point, every day, we had lunch at her house. Well, between not actually eating lunch and my workout, I lost a little weight. We never wanted lunch to end. We had great afternoons together. My bookkeeper Madge would call her house and tell us, "That's enough, children. Back to work."

Here is another story. There was a married girl who was always having problems with her husband. She had a body that would stop traffic. Well, this is true. She would walk out to get my lunch, and one day, she caused a major accident. She had tight pants on. I don't know how she even got them on. She was a hottie. We had plenty of fun and experiences together. She got me so hot one day the bookkeeper Madge literally told us to get the fuck out of the office and go get laid. Well, we both agreed— great idea—and we did. There was another secretary. Her name was Silvanna. She was crazily in love with me. She insisted to sit next to me in the office. She was so crazy she would just start making out with me in the office in front of everyone. My mom was working in the back office with Madge. Silvanna would call mom and say, "Yolanda, I just love your son." The funny part of this story was she was a bit older than me and was living with an roughneck Italian gardener. She couldn't tell him she wanted to leave him. She was scared of him, and he was paying all her bills. She wasn't convinced that I would take care of her and her bills. I don't know what it was with me. I had women like water, unbelievable. I had my spare tire down the shore. Debbie, aka the Debster, who worked in the area, would always stop by at work.

This next story was going to be told only because my friend Neil wants it included in the book. There was this neighborhood girl that would always stop by after hours. I don't remember how it started, but she would offer sexual favors. So I, Mr. Thoughtful, always thought of my friends. So one early evening, Neil came into the store. I kept the front door unlocked. He was dressed up as a roofer with a clipboard. He came directly to my office to find this girl totally nude. She was alarmed and nervous. Neil shouted out, "Well, Rich, how are you going to take care of the roofing bill? I asked you many times for the money." So I, Mr. Hollywood, had this scared look. I whispered into the girl's ear if she could take care of him. She was hesitant, and I begged her to help me. She then decided she would. I then explained to Neil how the bill would be paid in a low voice. We both had a very hard time containing our laughter, but we actually did. Well, we pulled it off. Another history lesson for the book. Then some time passed, and Neil understood what was going on in the fish palace, aka the whorehouse. I had a secretary who would perform different sex acts without any issues. She admitted she was a sex maniac. She flirted with some of the customers and even did some of them. Well, that's what I call customer security. They were not buying fish anywhere else. One day, she spoke to Neil on the phone and told him to come down and she would take care of him. Ten minutes later, he arrived, and he met her in the back office, and he was in heaven…*crazy stuff.*

Well, the business kept growing, and I even opened up another retail store. I had a lot on my plate. It was time for a road trip. The guys were getting itchy, and an opportunity came up. It was the old clam man, Billy. I knew Billy when I was a little boy and he was eighteen or nineteen, just starting his business. My dad was one of his first customers. Our relationship grew and also became very friendly. He invited me and my friends to come out to Long Island and party. Well, we sure did that. It was a buffet of goodies. There was plenty of green and white. We had a great time. That night, we headed over to one of the most popular clubs, the Obi. Well, let me tell you there was wall-to-wall action. We were all lit up, and it was time to work. Most of us hooked up that night. It was almost impossible not to. The fish were jumping in the boat. I did my part and met a real hottie that night. Actually, after that night, we exchanged numbers. I didn't want to fall into that long-distance driving story again. So we were able to set up a travel plan. She would take the LI train to Grand Central station in Manhattan, and I would pick her up from there. I would take her back to Jersey on my turf, and we would hang out either for some drinks or dinner then go back to my bedroom in my parents' house. Unfortunately, my room was over my parents' room. Of course, the floor would make noise, and I would be my father's topic of conversation to his buddies, how he had to hear me banging all night. We did this arrangement a couple of times. It didn't work especially during the week. I had to go to the Fulton market, and I wasn't going to drive to New York twice. The only solution was to bring her with me in the fish truck and drop her off at Grand Central before the market. I would park this stinky old fish truck in front and walk her in to the train stop. One early morning on Thursday, for some reason, the train wasn't coming for hours, and she was scared. She wanted me to wait with her. Well, I tried my best to comfort her and explain I need to buy my fish. Anyone who knows me would know I would always choose my business first. Well, I left this hottie in tears. She did not want to meet me anymore. Another story closed.

Trip to New York City and Fulton Market with Friend Neil

One afternoon, I received a phone call from my friend Neil. He asked me if I could help him out tonight, actually early morning. The night before, he had gone to New York City to see a concert, and his car broke down. It was stuck in New York. So he wanted to know when I went to the Fulton market in the morning if I could leave early with him to go on the west side of the city and help him get his car started. I agreed, so we did. That early morning, we headed out in this big, smelly fish truck to try to start his car. Unfortunately, we failed, so Neil ended up going to the Fulton fish market with me. He had to work that morning, so he thought he would sleep in the truck while I was buying dead fish. Well, we both were ball busters to each other. Today was my turn. He was trying to sleep, and I would throw ice at the truck window to wake him up. Then I put a dead mackerel on the windshield.

He was really pissed and tired. Well, I was finished, and we were headed back to New Jersey. We had one more stop in Jersey City at the Tunnel diner. We had to meet Billy the clam man. Well, we arrived, and I parked the truck and got out and met with Billy. Billy was all sad and teared up. I asked him what was wrong. He then replied John Lennon was dead. He was in shock. He was actually very depressed and mourning his death. So Nervous Nelly, aka Neil, started beeping the horn like a maniac. Billy was screaming to tell that idiot to stop. Billy screamed, "John Lennon is dead," no horn beeping. I proceeded to tell Neil this, so what does Neil did was beep more. I had to leave immediately. Billy was pissed.

New York Attack

This was a near-death encounter, another lifesaving event from God. This evening started out with me and two friends, Kevin M and Mike K. These two were like two sticks of dynamite. Once they got lit up, they would explode. The terminology *lit up* meant under the influence of major alcohol consumption and the white combo. To give you an idea, Mike K died of drug overdose, and Kevin M has lost most of his memory and is currently slicing deli meats with a college diploma.

This night was quite different. We were headed in to New York city for clubbing. Well, we hit a few different clubs, but unfortunately, there was no luck with the woman. The last club closed, and we were leaving on foot to our car parked a distance away. Well, Kevin and Mike were so wasted. I was the driver, so I took it easy. Mike was out of control as usual. He was embarrassing to be with, the comments that came out of his mouth. I suddenly distanced myself from them. There was a gang of Puerto Rican boys coming out of the club. Mike started shouting racial slurs to them. Five minutes later, the gang of four turned into eight Puerto Ricans. The next thing I saw, they were running after Kevin and Mike. They came to me to try to kill me. They questioned me if I was with them. I responded no. One of the Puerto Ricans said he had seen me with them. They knocked me to the ground and started to beat me. I then covered my face. They gave up and went after Kevin and Mike.

They finally caught them. Kevin and Mike got such a beating their faces were all busted up and bleeding. They were on the ground like a pancake that had been run over. I then picked each one of them up and put them in the car. Then I tried to help them, but they couldn't talk or move. These guys were in very bad shape. So I was on my way home and proceeded to the Lincoln tunnel when I was stopped at a light, not paying attention. The door opened on the passenger side, and this hot girl jumped in and said, "Hi, cutie, want to have a good time?" I was in shock with these two bleeding idiots in my back seat and this little hottie in the front. Thirty seconds later, she reached for my genital area. I then realized this was not a dream. She was a prostitute. I told her to get out and pushed her out. Well, I finally got these guys back to their homes. Both of them needed medical and dental attention. They couldn't eat normally for six months. They were sipping their food through a straw for six months.

Well, eventually, Dad had his first heart attack, which was inevitable. I saw him in the hospital. I was a grown man. I broke out hysterically crying. I knew his life was over soon. I did what I could to run his business while he was recuperating. He did not listen to anyone, doctors or family. He went right back to work and continued to go out on his pleasure boat fishing. Well, one Sunday, June 8, he decided to go out on his boat with his two friends, and one of them brought his girlfriend. Well, P.S. I guess, Dad had a massive heart attack on his own boat and died. He was brought into shore dead. The best thing was it was June 8, my birthday, and I was coming home on the Parkway and felt the vibe something was wrong. I called my house, and they broke the news to me: "Your father has died." Well, Dad died, and everything fell to shit.

Margaret finally got married. I walked her down the aisle as her father should have. Margaret and Gary paid for their wedding with their wedding envelopes. Then there was Richard and Merianne. I didn't know which end to turn to first. I had so much shit going on; it was a three-ring circus. I had a wholesale/retail market in Orange. I had a retail concession in Roseland. Now I had to take care of my father's retail/wholesale business. What would I do first? Stay calm and deal with it. I was teaching a very good friend of mine the business. I then set him up in my dad's store, and my Merianne also was going to help me out and run the store. The problem was my brother and mother wanted to keep my dad's business in the same format. I told them, "It is different now. You need to keep everything locked up and have tight inventory." With that said, I explained to Merianne she needed to watch everything and spend a lot of time there. Well, this was not her plan. She wanted to continue her lifestyle, get her nails done, go to the salon, and work out at the gym. We always spent holidays together with our families. Our families were so close I had even lent her brother Sal a large amount of money—that's how close we were. We were later talking about Sal coming in as a partner in the seafood business. Michelle, her sister, was even working in the office at the fish market. We would go on vacations in the Caribbean and enjoy good times together. On New Year's Eve, we would always go all out and go to one of those big hotel parties where you sleep over. We would go with my friend Neil and his girl. We would really party it up—mirrors ripped off the wall, bottles of liquor—you name it. We lived like there was no tomorrow. We would do the same in Atlantic City. We would party like crazy. Sometimes my buddy Joe Galinha would come down with us from Massachusetts. We would eat at the best seafood buffets. There was shrimp the size of your hands, king crab, you name it. I would gamble on the roulette. I would bring a brown bag filled with presidents. Those were the days. We had many arguments and a lot of tension built up between us. She became very sick and was having panic attacks. Now we had another problem; now she had appointments to counsel her. Well, more shit hit the fan—there was frozen seafood missing from the downstairs freezer. The money wasn't adding up. There was very good information that my good friend was helping himself. Next, there were rumors which usually were somewhat true—that my friend was feeling up my fiancée, Merianne, in the cooler. How true it was I will never know. But till this day, this guy has kept his distance from me. So I believe this is not rumor, probably true.

Well, the pressure was too much, and I began looking at life differently. My dad passed away at the age of fifty years old. He worked and worked, hoping to enjoy his older days in life. I didn't want to follow that same road. The difference was I wasn't smoking like a chimney and eating every meal like it was my last. I had plenty of exercise, which he didn't. So at least I had those things on my side for a longer life. Unfortunately, I still had his genes. This composure was very dangerous. We were both compulsive about different things. For example, he would go leisure fishing on his boat. He would bring large plastic garbage cans filled with ice out with him and whoever went fishing. He would not come back to port until they were filled with fish. It was a rare day. They would be empty or half-filled. If you went with him fishing, he would travel wherever it was needed. It could be one hour up to two hours just to get to the fishing grounds. If you were seasick, too bad, buster—he was not turning in. Your only hope was to pray to God it would be over soon and try to sleep. This was true. He was having a heart attack on his own boat and wouldn't turn in till he finally dropped dead on the floor. When it came to gambling, it was the same story. He wouldn't just play with what he could afford—he went over his head. Later on in the book, I will discuss where I come in with the compulsive features that ruined my life. The only differences I was able to see the problem and turn it around to safety.

Chapter 5D

I then sold my business to another wholesale fish dealer in Jersey city, M. Schact. I made a deal, which worked out for both of us. He purchased everything but the building, which I rented out. I then, as part of the deal, went to work for them. This was quite a venture. I met a lot of new people. I saw a lot of people I had known throughout the years. This company was big. The owner was an older gentleman with some knowledge of fresh fish but who mostly knew the frozen end of the business. I learned a lot of things. The owner, Murry Schact, took a liking to me. We got along great. He was a wonderful guy. He had a way with people; everyone liked him. If you had a problem, he would find a way to fix it. This business basically started at 1:00 a.m. to 8:00 p.m. There was so much going on and so many employees. Actually this business ran very efficiently. He had good employees who he had to pay. He would walk in to work at 10:00 a.m. after most of the action was over. I was totally amazed he would walk into a major fish company in a suit and tie. He proceeded upstairs and would do his frozen purchasing and go over the receivables and payables. I only saw him yell or talk loudly to his personal "slave," Jeff. Jeff would be in charge of doing all his personal chores. He would pick up his clothes at the cleaners, make dinner reservations, get his car maintained, etc. Jeff was his little puppy dog. Well, one day, there was a little conflict between the manager John and me. He felt under pressure with having me around. He was under the impression I would take his job. He was waiting for the right opportunity to get me out of there.

One night, Murry arranged a dinner get-together to discuss the future of the company and try to figure out the players. He was getting ready for retirement. Well, that night, present was myself, John M, Jerry M, Murry, and I believe Jeff F also. The dinner was great. Conversation was very upbeat until Murry suggested I start taking over some managerial duties from John. Well, John hit the ceiling. He screamed loudly at Murry, "Just let Rich do everything and fire me." He burst out in tears and ran out of the restaurant like a three-year-old having his tantrum. Well, the hatred and competition grew between us.

There was this really beautiful college girl. She was, I believe, Puerto Rican and worked in the office with Murry. I had the hots for her. I was finding excuses to go up to Murry's office to see her. I actually drove her home from work a couple of times. John was fuming every time I was up there. Well, he found his opportunity one day. I took an extended lunch with my gorgeous Cuban secretary whom I was dating. He made a big deal about taking extra time. I was not an employee on a set lunch schedule. He told me I was fired. Murry was on vacation in the Caribbean visiting some customers. John was left in charge of the ship. We had words, and it almost came to a fistfight. I left voluntarily.

Chapter 5E

Well, that was his biggest mistake. The war had begun. He had just let the hungry, angry lion out of his cage. My mom still had Dad's store open. Well, that afternoon, I started planning my strategy. I started contacting my old accounts and told them what happened. They told me they would support me. We all know how that works; it all revolves around money. Who would give them the better deal? Well, the war began. I started calling and getting orders. M. Schact started calling and not getting orders. They started lowballing the customers. Then things started rocking; the price wars began. Well, I started gaining ground. I ordered more trucks and built outdoor coolers and freezers. Then my brother-in-law Gary joined me. Things became crazy. We outgrew the location. There was absolutely no room. Well, what to do? I still owned my old warehouse in Orange. The produce company that was renting was closing their doors. It now became available. Perfect timing.

Chapter 5F

We made the move from Montclair to Orange. We were now the new Artie's Seafood. Well, the war did not slow down. I had a lot more room now. So I made up my mind and full blast ahead. My strategy was like a general at war. *How do you take the enemy down?* I started to hire their key employees. I started now taking their major accounts. I was on fire. My business was getting crazily busy. It was a good crazy. I was importing entire ship containers of shrimp from the far east. That was a situation in itself.

I would have to prepay with a letter of credit for the shrimp with a prearranged price. The shipment would arrive two months later. The shipment would arrive. It was mine, no returns, no credits given when it arrived. The process was it had to pass customers and FDA inspection. Many a time there was a problem with the product. It didn't pass FDA inspection. The only hope I would have was to beg the FDA to release the product to a certified lab to find out the exact problem and see if it could be corrected before the shrimp would get destroyed. Well, the labs would work with me and they would tell the FDA for this product to be salvaged, it would need to be cooked and sold as a cooked product, not raw. They accepted that method. I would take a big loss. One time, the shrimp company packed fish guts and squid heads in shrimp boxes and sent them to me. This was my importing business experience. I did not see much of a future in this. It was also very hard to get paid for the product. Some of these wholesalers were real deadbeats. I was exporting fish to wholesalers and hotels all over the Caribbean. I was selling to some of the major restaurants in New York City. I was supplying major airlines and cruise ships. Forget about it—I was number one in the area. Well, before this really got going, we were getting a lot of products direct from shippers. We were bypassing the Fulton fish market. This was not just happening with me, but a few other companies were doing the same. Well, this didn't go over too well with the seafood workers union and the delegate leaders, Dennis and Anthoney (Beansy). They had to put a stop to us. Well, they did to the weaker sheep. There were two bulls that didn't accept it. One was John S from Fulton Lobster Company, who would fight tooth and nail. He kept out of their way, and he made it very hard for them to stop him. One, day they were picketing outside his warehouse. John got so mad he chucked a full moon of his butt to Dennis and told him to kiss his ass. John S had balls of steel. We were competitors and friends in the past. Actually, John had worked at the Manor Restaurant when we were younger. One

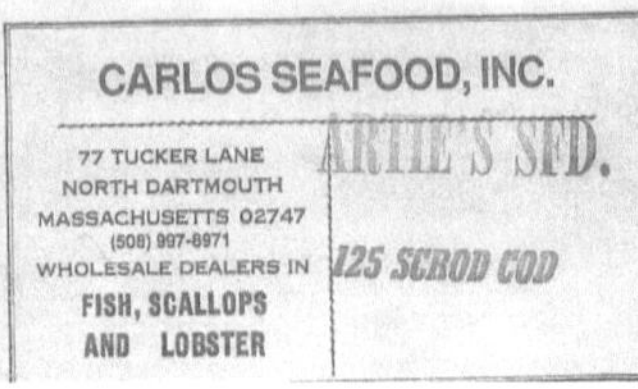

CARLOS SEAFOOD, INC.

77 TUCKER LANE
NORTH DARTMOUTH
MASSACHUSETTS 02747
(508) 997-8971
WHOLESALE DEALERS IN
FISH, SCALLOPS
AND LOBSTER

day, he came to my warehouse in Orange, New Jersey, and just walked right in my office and picked up my customer list. I then threw him out of my store. Ten minutes later, I look in my cameras and saw him in my garbage dumpster looking for information. What a crazy, ballsy guy he was. As years went on, he finally went out of business. The other sheep became victims of vandalism and death threats. Trucks burned down to the ground or wheels loosened from their trucks so they would fall off while driving, etc. Some companies such as Montclair Seafood would not get their truck loaded at the market until 10:00 a.m. That would prevent Montclair Seafood from providing good service to their customers. Some of these companies just gave in and became unionized. This would increase their costs greatly and make it hard to compete.

Well, now it came to me, little Richie, son of Artie, well-known throughout the market as a quiet little guy not getting into anybody's business. It started one day outside the market three blocks away. I would meet an Americana trailer truck to pick up some products I purchased directly. A jeep pulled up with tinted windows and jammed on the brakes. Vito, the driver of the trailer, looked at me, and we said to each other, "Who the fuck is this?"

Well, this big, brawly guy with shaded glasses popped up and said, "What do you think you guys are doing? You can't buy direct—everything has to go through the market."

I answered him, "Okay, thank you."

The following week, it was the same story, but this time, Dennis was pissed. He said, "I gave you your warning. If I see you again here, both of you guys will not be around anymore."

Next adventure, I started getting calls from Dennis and his associates how I needed to unionize my company. I was told it would be for everybody's good…if you know what I mean. Then he got Beansy involved. He didn't realize it was me. He started as a salesman in the market with Philly Cohen at T & S Fish Company. He remembered me as a little boy and was fond of Dad. When I asked for credit when I first opened from Philly, Beansy even got involved and told Philly, "He is a good kid. Give him a chance." Beansy got out of the situation. This was Dennis's deal. Well, I started rebelling against Dennis. Things were so crazy in that Fulton Market. I was this young, sheltered kid who had grown up in the suburbs of New Jersey. I didn't have any idea of crooks, gangsters, and hoodlums. This was all new to me. Well, there was a frozen fish company that sold frozen seafood at better pricing. The only catch was they didn't open up till 7:00 a.m. I had gone there many times. Well, one day, I pulled up to Alba Seafood on Water Street and park my truck in front, waiting for them to open shop. I had a full load of seafood in this big international box truck. I am sitting in the truck, listening to the AM radio, and this hoodlum proceeded to come to my window and leaned on the door so I can't see my mirror. His buddy was in the back of the truck trying to break in to it and steal my seafood. This guy is talking louder, and I hear the doors open in the back. He proceeded to try to keep me in the truck. My instincts told me something was going on. I then grabbed my longshoreman's fish hook and knocked this guy out of the way. I ran to the back and was able to stop the crime. Well that was quite an experience. The leader of the market carmine had bought a trucking company that I was using. One of the employees was helping himself to my product. I complained to one of the bosses. The next morning, I got such a beating from Frankie, the guy that was stealing from me. I was in the back of this big box truck with no lighting, stacking by hand hundred-pound fish boxes of fish and twenty-five pounds of ice in them. In those days, there were no forklifts, just hand trucks and hardworking men. He jumped up inside the truck and gave it to me good. I was in such pain I fell to the floor of the truck. I lay there in pain for a while.

The next morning, I pulled in to the market. Two guys were waiting for me. As soon as I got out of the truck, they grabbed me one by each arm and said, "Carmine is waiting for you."

I responded to them, "I need to buy a few things then I will meet him."

They responded, "No, you are meeting him now at Carmine's Bar and Grill." I was a little nervous. I was being dragged in to a secluded area with the godfather of Fulton Street, a kid of all. Well, here we were—Carmine sitting in a booth with the customized getup, the shaded glasses, etc. Well, he was quite a gentleman. He offered me a shot or a drink at 3:30 a.m., then out of respect, I had a rum and Coke.

Basically, he wanted to apologize for the beating I received yesterday, he told me he had no problem with me and Frankie would say he was sorry and he appreciated my business.

We shook hands, and he said, "Anything you need, reach out to me," and I left. That was it. I had had it. My dad came home that same week and had told my mother your son is in great danger. There are rumors of a contract out on him. He opened his mouth to the wrong people. Of course, this was exaggerated. I would get whacked that easy for some improper lip service. Well, I had been thinking about what to do and how to get out of this situation.

I remembered my Uncle Sam, aka the Buggy Man—this nickname was given to him when we were little kids. He would make these scary faces and sounds and scare the living shit out of us, hence came his name. He would always tell me, "Don't worry, if you ever have a problem, I know the right people." My daughter-in-law's brother was connected. I told my mom I was going to call Uncle Sam. I told him my problems, and I need his help ASAP. He then set up a meeting with me. His name was Larry. We met in Bayridge, Brooklyn, for a meeting. Larry was a tall, heavy-set, dark-haired man. He had the typical tinted glasses, black pants, black shoes. That all came along with the strong Brooklyn accent. Well, in those days, you just don't blend in or talk to these kind of people unless someone will make the guarantee that the person is legit. Well, my Uncle Sam did that for me. I was in. We had many meetings and different discussions. How would I benefit and what contributions would I be making? Well, our next meeting there was a brown bag exchange to Larry. He then distributed some of it to the captain. Larry was a lieutenant. This was the beginning of our agreement. One week later, the word reached the Fulton Market's family. I never had a problem or threat or disrespect again. I was actually looked at differently by some of the guys I had problems with. Even that piece of shit Dennis was saying "Good morning" to me. Well, things started going in the right direction. Now my trucks and fish were well-protected, and no one dared fuck with me again. Actually, I would be offered deals on the swag fish that were hustled through the night from the crew in the Fulton Market.

Well, my dealings with Larry were not over. They had just begun. Once you started, basically, there was no way out. Well, we had many meetings, and I was introduced to many different characters. So I sent Larry to visit my friend in Jersey. Larry started doing collections for me. I had such a large amount of customers. There were always some who only liked to receive and not give. Well, unfortunately, that didn't work in my business. Some of these people got the message clearly, and some didn't. The ones who didn't want to pay received some presents from Larry, and sometimes, they were forced to shut their businesses down for the night or longer, depending how long it took them to understand to pay up. Larry had his right-hand man, Paulie. These two guys would come over to the fish office every morning from Brooklyn. They would plan their activities for the  day, or sometimes it would be at night, depending on the situation when they could reach the money person. These two guys would like to talk first and try to rationalize with the customers. Sometimes it would be easier to make a payment plan than resort to step number two. Step two would include a full dining room of customers, and they would walk in as customers would be seated centrally. Then Paulie would go out to the car and bring in a large bag of white mice and release them in the dining room. Usually the restaurant would be frantic, ladies screaming, people running for the exits. No one would pay their bills. Or step three, they might get a fireworks display in the restaurant with M80s and smoke bombs. Basically, the same effect would happen with the diners in the restaurant. It would sound like a battlefield. The next day, the owner would get a visit or a phone call stating how unfortunate and terrible that was last night. "We were wondering if you had our payment ready?" If that didn't work, you can use your imagination what the next step was. That usually was the tipping point. In this time, my business was growing, but it could have grown more. I sent Larry to visit my friend John at M. Schact Seafood in Jersey City, the place where he threw me out in the street. At this time, the owner Murry Schact passed away and his wife was the owner with John running the place. Well, Larry visited him, and he opened his mouth with the wrong words. He caught a little beating in his office. At that point, Larry came back to the captain and reported what was going on, and this would be big. Well, they orchestrated sending in their own crew as workers. They basically bankrupted the company and took all the products. What I got out of this deal was I took over some of the major customers. So it was a win/win for everyone.

Years went by, and I was introduced to more and more of the family. They took a liking to me. I made money for them they made money for me. There would be weekly meetings with the family and crews at different locations that were controlled and guaranteed safety. There was a hotel with the restraint part would be used on a Friday night or a restaurant in Edgewater or in Staten Island or Brooklyn. There was usually a different location each week, which was disclosed at the last minute. At these gatherings would be a lot of envelopes switching hands and mostly ending up in one pile of the bosses. I had built up trust for myself. I proved I was one of them. I was on their side. They invited me to many meetings and dinners. There were plenty of Atlantic City trips in the limos, visits to some of the after-hours and social clubs. I was on my way to being a soldier. I turned the family on to many adventures of fortune. They had my trust and honor through the old-time ceremony and rituals. My wholesale seafood business was incredible. We were known as New Jersey's largest dealers. We were serving some of the highest-end restaurants in New York. We supplied all three of the major airports. We also supplied cruise ship lines and major supermarket chains. We exported container loads of fish to all over the Caribbean. Believe it or not, I was shipping fish to England. This fish market was rocking. We were open twenty out of twenty-four hours a day seven days a week. We were receiving tractor trailers from the New England area and from down south. We had five Portuguese top fillet cutters with a skinning machine. They would be cutting fish all night long. All this was against and not allowed by the fish union. I had no problem anymore. I didn't have to answer to anybody. I had my pass, and that's it. No disruptions or questions. I have a couple of office stories I wanted to include in the book. One was John. He was a bookkeeper we hired to help out. John was a very polite, quiet guy. He didn't match with the other male employees. He was a gentile guy, didn't have any signs of craziness. Well, after hours he was a different guy. He was dating a black girl with five kids. He was lost and confused. One day, he came in and was acting very strange. He actually went outside and climbed up in one of the big trucks and was looking in to the mirror and was having a full-blown conversation with the mirror. We needed to get him help. That was the end of John, committed to the crazy house.

Another story was our two salesmen—we had Bill Clark and Buddy. First, we will talk about Buddy. He was a grouchy, old, boisterous man trying very hard to make a living selling fish. He would attack the phones nonstop and be persistent in his sales approaches. His brakes would consist of smoking. One day, he was really wired up on his coffee. My cousin Steve grabbed some fresh squid out of the cooler and managed to put it on Buddy's chair. Buddy finally sat down and felt the squid ink hit his clothes and go through to his body. He didn't know what was happening. He was on the phone with a customer. He stood up and screamed. (They were fucking with me as I spoke.) Everyone in the office couldn't believe what Steve did. We also had Henry in the office, and my right-hand man, Mikey. Mikey did everything for me. He did whatever in the fish

business; he did things for me in my rental business; he was an Italian kid from Belleville. He was a street kid. We had become friends. His trust was proven. He then was allowed to hang out with the crew. Later on, he was involved in some of our other side businesses.

Well, time has passed, and I was working very hard, and I also was divorced from my first wife for quite a while now. I was making very good money. I was buying multifamily houses in the Orange, New Jersey, area and renting them out. Unfortunately, the crowd was not the most desirable tenants. I had incurred many problems. My experience grew very fast. There were people that wouldn't pay their rent and do damage to the apartments. It was becoming overwhelming for me. Most of the times, either at eviction from the court or before the sheriff came, they would just abandon their clothes, furniture, etc. I would have to get some of my employees from the fish market to empty the apartment in one of my trucks and fill up an entire dumpster with all this garbage. This was not just once; it became a regular thing.

Another story was this one lady was so backed up on the rent; she knew all the tricks how to keep postponing the eviction. This one pulled there was lead in the paint, and it was unsafe for her and her family. The judge ordered testing on the windowsills and door frames. The house was old. These items were the only items that were never replaced. Well, there was a very small trace of lead present. We were in the court for the eviction hearing. I brought forward all the facts. I had not been paid for over four months, and there was serious abuse and damage to the house. I also told the judge she should have been evicted months ago. Well, he did not like my answers and tone. He stated, "One more word out of you, you will be in contempt of court and will be going to jail." I then shut up, and he gave his ruling. The ruling was for me to renovate all the windowsills and all the door frames and anything else that might have any lead presence. In the meantime, the tenant and her six children will be put up in a hotel at their expense until the job was completely done and had certification from a licensed lead inspector. As far as your past due rent was concerned, if by the time she moves back in to your home and it is not paid, you need to file for eviction again. How do you like that? Unbelievable. The last deciding factor for selling all this real estate was a very scary story. Well, here we go. I knocked on the door of one of the tenants to collect an overdue rent. She invited me in, and from nowhere, this shady-looking, drugged, and drunk black guy jumps out at me with a gun. He then proceeded to tell me, "We ain't paying you. What are you going to do about it, white boy?" Meanwhile, he was pointing a gun at the back of my head. I did not freak out or do anything stupid. I didn't know if the gun was loaded. I then tried to rationalize with him; that didn't work. I then told him two people were waiting for me who he doesn't want to meet. Luckily, Larry and Paulie were at the fish market. If I am not back in ten minutes, you and your girl were done. His girl talked to him to put the gun down and leave her house. Well, that was a close one, but after that, I decided to get the hell out of this area.

Chapter 5G

Well, I figured maybe I can open up again, on a smaller level with just a few accounts. This would keep me occupied and out of trouble. Also, a few bucks never hurt anyone, so it was perfect timing. The old company closed up, and I opened a small operation. It still was a lot of work. I couldn't get my fish delivered. I was on a smaller scale than before. Every morning, I went down to Fulton Street and picked up my load of fish. I did start to order some fish directly when the business grew a bit. It was dropped off at South Street. It was okay. I had a different outlook on the business. I was friendlier with my employees. I treated them very good. As a matter of fact, one of them to this day is one of my best friends. We have a very special bond of trust and friendship with each other. I gave Brian a lot of responsibility, and he proved to me. We were brothers; we did everything together. What we didn't do. I was still single and went out sometimes during the week but definitely on weekends. This next story will really get you. I became like the father in church, Father Consolor. When I would go out to these go go bars. I would have deep, intense conversations with these girls. I would shame them why they would do this kind of work. What if their families knew about this? Well, I would convince them to come to work with me in the fish market. Yes, there were a couple of them that did. Some of them wouldn't listen or care for anything in this world. They just wanted those big bucks. The ones that wanted to join me would pack orders, clean squid, etc. They were happy and had a piece of mind again. Yet some of them would turn back to the crazy life of go go dancing. Most of them, I think, made the change for me. They all fell in love with my kindness and caring and respect for them. I had relationships with them. It was quite an experience for both of us.

There was one girl, Lana. This girl was so deeply in love with me. She would do anything for me. I had a dispute with her one day. I don't know if you knew some of the Brazilians believe in *ma cumba* voodoo. Well, just my luck—she was deep into it. She went to her friend's house one day after she was so upset with me. Her friend Lee must have been the voodoo doctor. Well, they told me I was doomed until I fixed the situation with Lana. I just laughed and went on living. Well, the next day, it started happening. I had disaster after disaster. I had things happen that you couldn't believe. This happened for one week straight. I gave up. I went down to Newark and made peace with Lana. Believe it or not, there were no more problems or disasters. Well, is voodoo real? That's for you to find out. I believe it is. This was no coincidence, not the amount of events that took place. Well, I had a lot of interesting people working for me. I had a college kid who used to work for me years ago. He seemed to me as an honest, hardworking kid. He worked for me one summer, and I gave him responsibilities of loading the trucks. Well, my judgment was wrong; he was ripping me off with two of the drivers. They were putting extra fish on the truck, and the driver would sell it, and they would split the money. Well, I caught all three of them one day and fired all of them. I was still in contact with the Family. Larry and Paulie, and the crowd started growing more and more. Well, I believe at this time, the feds were trying to round up the different families and try to put an end to it. Guiliani did a pretty good job of cleaning up the Fulton market. Well, in all this hustle and bustle, they were trying to find angles to have every one turn on each other.

One day at my home, the doorbell rang. I looked outside and saw a black sedan car unmarked. I said to myself, "The day has come." Well, lucky for me, one of my Brazilian friends was over. She answered the door, and a guy in a trench coat told her he needed to speak with Richard H.

She then called me, and I went to the door and asked him, "Can I help you?"

He said, "I need to speak with Richard H."

I then responded, "That's my dad—he is not here now." This fed agent did not look like he had too much intelligence. Well, he bought it and handed me a card for the main FBI office in Newark and told me to have my dad call them. Well, I called them the next day, and they wanted to meet with me and discuss some information they had on me. I don't know what happened, but they power-played me. They froze all my bank accounts and access to my safe deposit box. I called the bank, and they told me there was a court order from the United States government to freeze all assets from me.

I called the feds again, and they said, "That's just the beginning. We need you to meet with us and tell us about your involvement and a list of other people."

I had received some advice to contact this high-profile

lawyer. He dealt with these types of cases. Well, I did hire him. It was beyond costly, something like $750 per hour. I had no choice but to pay the piper. Well, I had rights, and I wasn't singing under any circumstance. I knew nothing. I was an honest businessman in the seafood business. Well, they were able to prove some cash transactions and the frequency of changing smaller bills into hundred-dollar bills. The moral of the story is I got off with a very large legal bill, a warning from the feds that they would be watching me and my actions very carefully. "There will be no next time. You will go directly to jail on Rico charges, and all your funds will be confiscated." Well, this was kind of the separation between the Family. I kept far away from Larry and the crew. They were hot on my trail. It was easy to fry up all the little fish first then go after the whale. I heard rumors they were splitting up among themselves and getting different styles haircuts, dying their hair different colors, etc. Everyone was just being careful. They did pick up some of the crew, but there was plenty left behind them.

Time went on. I was getting tired and burnt out again. I decided to sell out again. I became interested in the financial world. I wanted to work on Wall Street. Well, that would be quite a challenge since I didn't have a college education. I had the opportunity to go to college, but I declined. I took all the preparatory classes in high school and was ready. I spoke with some old-timers, and they said there were quite a number of stock brokers without a college education. I had a mouthpiece worth a million dollars. I could sell the Brooklyn Bridge if I had to. In the financial business, that's what counts: your sales ability, opening accounts and raising money. I then found a boutique firm not far from my home. They gave me a chance because of my sales background. Well, here we went—another business with drama. You couldn't just be a stockbroker. You needed training and multiple laundry lists of financial licenses to be obtained. Well, I started off at this major firm a grown man going to work in a suit and tie. My career started in the mail room, a job an eighteen-year-old would start at. I was opening mail, putting postage, and sending out brochures, also assisting the senior brokers. In the beginning, it was humiliating for me. As time grew, I became friendly with the brokers. They would pass over to me some hot tips that I would act on in my own account. Well, after four months, they sent me to financial school on Wall Street to train for my licensing. I then passed a series of different tests for my licenses. I moved on to another firm. Well, it started getting crazy. I was involved with some real characters. This firm was like you would see on TV. There were so much goings-on it was crazy. Actually, one of the brokers was sent to jail. I happened to notice him fifteen years later selling mattresses at Sleepies. This time was the Internet craze. You can put names of companies in a hat and pick anyone. They would all go up. I was making good money in my own account. I also had some high-end clients. I would make the clients sometimes twenty or thirty thousand dollars a day. Internet stocks were exploding. I moved on to another firm, which had different branches in New Jersey and in Manhattan. I worked at all three of them. I couldn't believe what was going on. I had a book of some customers. I was making a fortune in my own account. I just started in this business, and I couldn't believe it. I was actually a person again. I didn't smell like a baccala anymore. I didn't eat leftovers and didn't wear old, smelly fish cloths anymore. I also didn't wake up at 2:00 a.m. either. I went to work with a Brooks Brothers suit and tie, ate lunch at some of

the finer restaurants, and worked eight to five, five days a week. Every day without fail, the cash register rang. Well, how long would this last?

I decided to take a vacation. I met up with one of my Brazilian girlfriends. She invited me to her house in Brazil. She had a brother, and we became friends. We went on many day trips throughout the state. This guy made a new meaning for the words *crazy times*. He had the upper hand on the trips. Since he spoke the language fluently and he knew the roads and the hot spots, he always had first pick of the crop. Well, that was okay; it all was good. What he left and wasn't his first pick was a diamond in the rough for me. You didn't hear me complain. We met two lovely, educated girls. They were sisters. I started dating one and became serious with her. At this time in my life, I really wanted to settle down and have a family. She had the same hopes. Well, she became my wife. Unfortunately, I was ready to start this new dream life with all good intentions, and the stock market blew up. It finally happened—the tech bubble popped. The music stopped, and there were no more chairs for me to sit

Musical Chairs

Everything went to hell in a handbag. I was leveraged up the kazoo on a margin, borrowed money from the brokerage company. I was all in, selling puts, long equities, the whole deal. Well, that day, the market tanked. I was in a margin call. I was out of emergency money, and my equity dropped to a major disaster. I was either going to take a very big loss on a sellout from the margin department or I had one last hope. My brother had plenty of money available. I asked him for a loan so I could pay off my margin call. He refused me. He didn't feel comfortable doing it. He thought it would be putting more fuel on the fire. I tried to explain it would save my account. Well, if I had had that loan, it would have saved my account. The market started rallying back, and my equity would have risen. Instead, my account was sold out and dwindled down to nothing. That day, I never experienced such a feeling of sadness, emptiness, and depression. I actually cried like a three-year-old. I was devastated by what just happened. Years and sweat and torture were all lost within one session of the stock market. My life had just changed. I had all kinds of bills; my brokerage customers took a hit. No one wanted to invest or open any new business. Since this was a commission paid job, that meant I was going hungry. I couldn't trade anymore because my money was gone.

Well, time was passing, and nothing was changing except more bills. I had to find a way to produce money fast. I did. It was good, old-fashioned hard work. I started my own driveway sealcoating business. I started making pamphlets and advertising in the local newspaper. I started getting calls. It  was amazing. I would go give the customers estimates. Some of them would complain the price was too high. I would use my sales experience and explain to them the quality of work they would receive. Most of them were sold on my sales pitch. I had plenty of work. The best thing with this business was there was little to no investment to do this business. It was mostly labor involved. This was working out great. I would do it on weekends and sometimes call in sick at the brokerage firm. I didn't want to give up the brokerage job. I believed things would get better soon. Well, it didn't get better, just my bills got bigger. I then saw an advertisement for a fish cutter. I applied for the job and took it. Well, now I was really committed to work. This job was from 10:00 p.m. till 7:00 a.m. I then would rush home, take a shower, and race in my car down to the brokerage job in Islen, New Jersey, for 9:00 a.m. I would work all day and arrive home after 6:00 p.m. I would eat dinner and try to sleep a couple of hours till I had to go to the fish job. On Saturdays and Sundays, both jobs were closed. Well, you would figure, Perfect, I can recuperate and rest. No, that was not part of the vocabulary. On Saturday and Sunday, I would do sealcoating of driveways. Well, I was working seven days and paying bills. This picture didn't make sense. Something was wrong. Yes, I would be driving to the brokerage firm every day, using all kinds of gas, tolls, and wear and tear on my car. I also needed to buy lunch. Well, things were still bad, no commissions. This job was actually costing me money instead of making money.

Chapter 5H

I finally started thinking something was wrong. I needed to fix it. I needed to find some steady work where I could make some big bucks and get back on the top again. Well, after two weeks of hemming and hawing, going back and forth in my thoughts, I decided, *Well, I always did very well in the fish business.* I just couldn't face starting from zero and facing my suppliers, friends, etc., again. I thought I was free and clear and didn't have to deal with that smell, crazy early hours, and crazy people. Well, I decided I would go back to the fish business. I was flat broke. I had to take a loan out for a down payment on a van and working capital. I then proceeded to go to the GMC dealer and order a brand-new refrigerated van. It was two weeks in after I ordered the van.

Another setback happened in my life. It was September 11. The world had now totally changed overnight. No one knew what would be. What just happened to their future and the future of the country? I again was in utter shock. There was nowhere to run, nowhere to hide. I just personally signed and gave a large deposit on a van. I had no source of income and nothing but more bills. Well, I had to step up and face the music. This was a lot more than I had bargained for. New York's Fulton fish market was located in the heart of the war zone in lower Manhattan. It was being moved to a makeshift market in a large parking lot located in the Bronx. That would mean driving very far in uncharted waters. I never heard nothing but horror stories of Huntspoint. I didn't know what to expect. I don't scare easy, but this time, there was some fear. There were many traffic lights where there were groups of people congregating in the middle of the night in the streets. Let's not forget there were panhandlers, prostitutes, drug dealers—you name it; you would see it. My van doors were locked and foot on the gas pedal ready to speed away. I was also riding with a pocket full of cash since I was just starting out again. I was the perfect target. Well, I had no warehouse. I was cutting fish and preparing my orders in the back of my van. I had a small chest freezer in my basement in my house. I also had a little office in my basement. It actually was a nice little setup. I did my own thing, no pressure, and a lot of hard work. I worked hard. I would buy my own fish, process it, and deliver it. I had really good relationships with my customers. I learned when dealing face to face, there was no bullshit. They wouldn't return anything or say anything was short on weight, and most important, I was paid. The business kept growing bigger and bigger. There was no more room in the van. Every day, it was filled from front to back. Most of the time, I would end up unloading half the van to find something. Here we went again. I found a garage-type building in an industrial park not far from my home. I rented it out. This meant more expenses, and I needed more business. I then ordered more trucks. I then furnished this space into a wholesale seafood company. It was ready to go. I hired drivers. This meant no more deliveries for me. I stayed in the store and packed up the orders and would be calling all day long for new business. The business became bigger. My wife decided to help me. We hired a fellow who helped cut fish and would work in the office helping me. We then hired a full-time bookkeeper. We must have had five trucks and about seven or eight employees. I totally had it under control. My expenses were livable, and

I was making money again. Well, before you knew it, I did it. I was back on top after about six years. My net worth grew where I needed it to be. Working without any partners or manager was tough, no vacation time. If I was sick, I had to work. There was a time I pulled my back out. I was stiff like a wood board in pain. I had to get up and go to the Fulton market in lower Manhattan. By the way, time had passed and all the damage in lower Manhattan at the market was repaired and they reopened the old market again. The future plans were taking place in Huntspoint of a state-of-the-art, new fish market.

Well, back to the story. My wife literally lifted me into the truck, and I drove off. When I finally got to the market, I couldn't even get out to do my buying. I ordered everything from the parking lot. There were times I had a terrible fever or cold; that didn't stop me from my responsibilities. I was a bull; nothing could stop me or kill me. Well, I have another highlight in this episode. Every night, we would pull in the box truck in the building and park in front of the walk in freezer. Well, usually, my wife would do it while I was closing everything up for the night. She had her little white boots on. One night, as she pulled the truck in, her boots were greasy or wet, and her foot slipped and hit the gas pedal. She went flying into the freezer and basically knocked down two of the four walls. This was on a Friday night. That was my only freezer, and it was late and every possible place I could bring it was closing. I had a mess. I had to think quick. Luckily, I found someone at preferred freezer in Perth Amboy, New Jersey. He would wait for us to bring all the frozen products. This was one of my deciding factors to cash out again. Problems were always a factor in this business.

Chapter 51

Well, time is going on, and there is no one to play with. Everyone is working; no one is retired or even semi-retired. I started getting bored. My good friend Rich told me about his first cousin. He was in the seafood business and his boss just died. He said the business was going in different directions and was not stable anymore. He wanted out. My friend suggested we get together and see if we can work something out. Well, I thought about something small and with a partner. With a partner, it really would not be that bad. The responsibilities and cost would be equal. There was the trust part—two complete strangers joining hands in this marriage of partnership. This combo was linked by one mutual person who was my friend Rich and his cousin. Well, Rich was old-school Italian like me. There is a bond of trust and a man's guarantee. Rich made the guarantees to both of us: to me that his cousin wouldn't steal from me, and for his cousin that I wouldn't steal from him, and every time I touched anything that dealt with fish, it turned to gold. Well, you will hear full details of the success of the company and how his cousin Rich made him a millionaire. Rich did not receive a brokers fee or commission on putting this deal together. I thanked him for my part. His own cousin did nothing, not even a thank-you, a lobster dinner, nothing. What an ungrateful, selfish person.

Well, we started. We both put up money and ordered three trucks and rented out a location in South Jersey. Again, starting out with nothing was not easy. In the beginning would be a lot of hard work and hours. We started the business. It was really tough starting out with one customer and each day growing. Well, it caught on. We started getting busy. We hired more employees. This part became very interesting. One of our first employees was an ex-convict on parole. This guy was very sincere and regretful for what he did. He was very reliable and trustworthy. He told us from day one he would never let us down and he would be with us forever. Well, he was right. He was with the company over ten years and retired. This guy made such an impression on us. We were asked from the chief of parole if we would hire more ex-convicts. We did try more. It was a win-win situation. They couldn't steal product or money from us. They couldn't call out sick or miss work. They had to drive safely and respect and not fight with anyone. These were all my downfalls with drivers in my past businesses. Also, the best part was they would be paid minimum wage and were happy with that. This form of labor did nothing but boost profits and grow the business. It was time for a vacation. I took off some time. I was basically the leader because I had the most experience and the only pair of balls in the place. When I came back, the business was in turmoil. I realized my partner was not acting as an owner. The business was neglected. There were very little orders. All the bookkeeping was screwed up. It came to roost that my partner was a very shy and timid individual. His communication skills were little to none. He couldn't have a simple conversation, much more talk to existing or prospective customers. It was just a mess that was left for me. Well, I surely didn't need all this bullshit. I was just looking to make a few bucks and keep myself busy. Well, like my mom always said, "People don't change. The situation is the only thing that can change." Thanks, Mom. I will never forget those words. Well, that was my cue to get the hell out. Things would not get better, and I would be held captive there without vacations. I decided to sell my partnership out. I was always receiving cards in the mail from business brokers. So what the hell? I called them up. We had a very encouraging conversation on the phone. He came down, and we went over the details. I came up with a big number for my shares. The broker went with it. He immediately received many phone calls. Wow, it was amazing. There were many prospective buyers. I received some good money for my shares and inventory, etc. I was home free. All of a sudden, I heard my partner changed over like a light switch. He finally took charge and acted like an owner should. He had no choice but to take these actions. When we started the business, his beginning money was a second mortgage on his house. He was married and had a kid. He had to save his business or he would be homeless. His new partner had no experience. He was very slow in learning anything. Actually, deep down, he really didn't want to learn. He was just mesmerized with the numbers like the rest of my past buyers. It seemed to be the same MO with these buyers. They were clueless about the business itself. This new partner would do nothing correct—nothing but mistake after mistake. My ex-partner was getting more aggravated and nervous each day. It got to the point he was cursing out his new partner and throwing fish products at him. I forgot to mention when I was involved previously in the business, I brought on a person that had fish experience to help us. He just went bankrupt for the second time and screwed a lot of people. He was glad to go down south to our business. He was low key trying to keep off the radar for his safety and embarrassment. Well, he was a big help for my ex-partner without me being there. With all the confusion with his new partner, he made the new partner sell shares to the helper. Three years went by, and things were getting a little better but still a mess. It was too much stress and work for my ex-partner. He asked me if I wanted to come back. I joined them again. I helped them build up the business. I was a partner again. The business grew nicely.

Chapter 6

Time Period from First Divorce to Second Marriage

I was in my mid-thirties; I was sitting pretty. I had a successful business. I was strong and handsome. I was partying every weekend. I would go out clubbing all the time. I started to show some high class. I mean first class. I went out and bought a 944 Porsche. I had fancy Brooks Brothers clothes, etc. Now I needed to fill the part. I started to go out to the high-end nightclubs.

One night, I met this Italian American girl; her name was Ann. Wow, she was so shy hanging out with her girlfriend that night. I walked up to her that night and started conversation with her. She was divorced with no children. She was very easygoing. She was very attractive and a real guidette. She was just what the doctor ordered. Wait, not so fast. Nothing is as good as it seems. We started dating and enjoyed each other's company immensely until her true colors came out. She loved to drink and do drugs. She would get so drunk she couldn't control her actions. I would end up carrying her out of a restaurant or a party. It was getting ridiculous. She used to smoke, which would make me sick. Well, I would always complain. The sex was amazing. We were very compatible except for when she would get trashed.

One day, we went for a ride to north Haledon, New Jersey, with that beautiful Porsche. I must have been going a little fast. I was pulled over by a cop. I was very calm. I didn't panic. He asked me for my driver's license, registration, and insurance card. I gave it to him, and he went to his car and wrote me out a ticket. He came back and gave me the ticket. He then told me to slow down next time. I was so glad it was over and he didn't call up headquarters to check on my license. Back in those days, everything was so slow, and it seemed like people were more stupid than these days. My concern was I was driving with a revoked license. That was not my first time doing that. I actually lost my license. I believe it was two times. My secret was when my license came due I, would always keep my expired license. When I would lose my license, I would send in the expired license to motor vehicle. Lucky me, the state of New Jersey would only hire complete idiots. They never noticed the expiration date. So I would be driving around with an updated current license even though it was revoked. Well, I had nerve like you couldn't believe to pull this off on two different times in my life. My girl Ann used to love all this mischievous doings of mine. She would get so turned on by my shady dealings in the fish business, meetings with the Italian boys, etc. She loved the fast life, fancy high-end cars, Lincoln town car, limos, the fancy clothes, Atlantic City trips.

When I was in my mid-twenties, I was pulled over down the shore in my Cadillac after leaving one of the nightclubs. I had my windows closed waiting for the AC to kick in. Meanwhile, the inside of the car smelled of alcohol. I was pulled over for a traffic stop. I pulled my window down, and the cop smelled the alcohol. He told me get out of the car. Then he started to give me some DWI exercises, which were totally ridiculous. I couldn't have even passed his test if I was straight. He was not pleased with my attitude and performance. He then said, "You are under arrest," and handcuffed me and took me in his police car to the station. My car was then towed to the police yard. They threw me in a cell like a prisoner. I had no one to call. I then called my girlfriend, Merianne, and she came down with her sister and bailed me out. We then headed home. I could not drive, so Merianne drove my car home. Well, this would be real trouble for me—I would really have problems. I hired an attorney who knew how to handle these types of cases. The bottom line was there were some envelopes exchanged, and the DWI charges were dropped to a two-point ticket.

There is one more police story. Many years later, I went to my friend Rich's bachelor party. I was so wasted. I was driving home in a rural area of Morris County. I happened to get lost. There was very poor street lighting and few signs on this dirt road. I was driving a little fast. There was a cop car hidden in the bushes, sticking out a little on the road. I almost hit the police car by accident. They came after me like a bat out of hell. Again, they smelled slightly of alcohol. They impounded my car and brought me in to the station to arrest me. I then started my usual verbal convincing that I couldn't see the rural road due to poor lighting. They didn't buy any of my stories. I then pulled out a PBA card and went that route. They were hemming and hawing, so I needed to reach deeper. I had one card left of the game of luck—that I was friends of a friend that was chief of police of a nearby town. Well, my luck was with me again. My friend called his friend, Chief Brian, then called the sergeant where I was being held. They had a brief conversation, then they told me they wouldn't arrest me. I could leave by someone driving me home. "You can pick up your car in the morning. You are free to go." Wow, how the hell did that happen?

I had a nice pile saved up. I decided to look at life differently. I spoke to my accountant and told him I was thinking of selling. The very next day, I received a call from him. He had a buyer with money. We then began to negotiate and made a deal. I was out. I stayed a while for the transition of ownership. I began to relax, go on several trips, etc. I also was still young and, at this point, single and divorced. I felt my oats again. I was single and free. I still carried on my life as a responsible, respectful businessman. But I still had the other side of me coming back like the good old days. I used to play the field at night. I would go out with some of my single friends like Brian N, Tony B, Paulie L, and Richie G. We would try to hang out at the club scene, but that wasn't really happening at our age. We discovered go go bars where we would frequent these bars in Newark, Paterson, etc. We had little problems in the beginning of this new adventure, then we learned how the system works. The girls we would target on were Brazilian. We had a good time since I knew how to speak some Portuguese with my friend Tony B. Most of the dancers were Brazilian. I was a big hit since I could communicate with them a little. Yeah, they thought they hit the jackpot. They would hope that they would be able to marry me or one of my friends for legal status. Unfortunately, we were well aware of that. That was not even a possibility. We just wanted to have a good time with them. I met quite a few of these girls. Some of them were real scum and were dirty whores who only cared about money. They were on a mission to make as much money as possible and as fast as possible. These group of animals would work seven days a week on double shifts. Some of them became alcoholics and drug addicts. The reason for this gold rush was the currency conversion. In Brazil, they use reels. In the USA, we use dollars. You would get many more reals for a dollar. So these girls were not paying taxes in Brazil or USA. This was all tax-free cash. Their expenses were limited. They would just need a place to sleep and store their suitcase of clothes. There would be three or four girls that would chip in for a small cheap apartment. Their meals would consist of a small, round aluminum container with rice, beans, salad, and either a small piece of meat or chicken. This was very cheap. Well, getting back to the other half of the Brazilian girls. There were some that were very sincere and honest. They also were on a mission, but they still believed in Jesus and the love of their families. All the dancers lied to their families. They would tell them they were working in a store or working as a secretary or something respectful. Meanwhile, they would be sending all kinds of money back to Brazil each week. Most of these girls came from small towns and countries. The families and friends would think that USA was heaven. They were saints with their families. When they got involved with this go go business, they were traumatized. They couldn't do such a thing. Their fellow workmates or girlfriends would remind them of the money. These girls would need to drink or do drugs to give them the courage to dance in a bikini in front of strange men in a dark bar late at night. Most of these girls got hooked on drinking or drugs. These beautiful girls started getting old-looking with wrinkles in the face and big circles around their eyes. This life took a toll on them. This is where my friends and I came in. We would play the part with them. There was dollars growing on trees, and Americans are all very rich. Some of the girls would have a lot of explaining to do, and some of them would have to come clean. Sometimes there would be some girls that would go to the USA and under any circumstance would or could not be a go go girl. They would then try to be a house cleaner or another low-paying job. Or some guys would go there to work in construction. If any of these non-go go people returned to these small towns, they would explain why they did not make boatloads of money like the other girls that were dancing. They were planning their future. If they live to see their future in Brazil. We just wanted to be friends with them and didn't show them a sexual interest in front of them. Even though that was complete torcher sitting next to them smelling their cheap ten-cent whore perfume, also having their huge breasts staring at you almost out of their tops and a tight little bottom exposed through their bikini. Believe me it took a lot of patience, but in the long run, it would be worth the wait. The friendship and trust grew. Soon they would let us drive them home, maybe stop at a dinner. We would take them out for lunch and dinner. They became very comfortable with us. There were big parties they would invite us to. Take us to the beach and let us put suntan lotion on them, and they would do the same for us. Then some of the situations became more serious. Some of them would date us, boyfriend and girlfriend. Some of the situations were even more serious. They would move in with us. Wow, that was the ultimate jackpot. Then again, you know how it goes. Once the hunter goes out, he is excited. When he catches his prey, the excitement is over. So after a while, it became too monotonous. Time to change the scenery. This wasn't too hard because your name was out there, and all the girls knew you and what they can have. There were plenty of prospects. We were like celebrities just as long as we did the right thing and didn't make a bad name for ourselves. This life became stale. It was going nowhere. How long could I go on keeping long hours, waking up early, and working hard? It was aging me as well. I knew I couldn't do this forever. I wanted to settle down with a nice girl. I did not have a go go girl in my dreams as a future wife. It was all good and fun. I was so close to one of the girls. Her stage name was Michelle. No one used their real names. They all had this fantasy life that no one from Brazil should discover. They told their families they worked completely different jobs and went to church once or twice a week. Once in a while, there was a blimp in the system. Someone from their town would discover them and go back to Brazil and start the rumors in the town. Most of the time, this fantasy would never be discovered.

Well anyway, Michelle had moved back to Brazil with her bank account filled. We were still friends and communicated on the phone. She invited me to Brazil to her house to stay. She knew I would keep the code of silence. We were very good to each other. I took a trip out there and stayed with her family. Her brother and I became close and started going out each day

and night. This guy was no saint, actually the opposite. He was such a whore master. He knew all the ladies, how to sweet-talk and bullshit them. Well, that was fine for me. Every day, we had a different girl to pick from. There was one day we had two girls each that day, the a.m. shift then the p.m. shift. Only one problem with him he was very greedy. He always had first pick of the litter. That was fine—I guess that is how it worked. I was not complaining—the second choice was still considered a hottie. After our nightly adventures, we would head back to the house. My sleeping arrangements were in Michelle's bed. I guess that was acceptable to the family. I can only imagine what she told the family who I was. Well, when I entered the bed, Michelle wanted her turn. Well, at that point, I was done. She wouldn't accept that. She brought things back to life.

One day, we took a trip for a week to another area. We were located in a mountainous, rural area. On our travels, we drove through very interesting small, poor towns where we traveled over wood plank bridges with the car and drove through towns where the children were so poor they had no clothes on. We traveled through farm areas where we saw cows that were stolen from the farms and slaughtered in the woods for their meat. It was an amazing experience to see how the other side lived. This trip was when I met my second wife and her sister. This became a completely different situation from our other adventures. These girls were different. They were educated and came from good families and had good jobs. There was no easy time with these two. We went out a few days and became bonded. I had to leave for USA. We kept in contact through the phone. We then spoke about future plans. She decided to come to USA and start a life with me. She came out, filed for a visa, and stayed with me for a while. We then decided to marry and eventually have a child together.

Chapter 7

My Married Life with Children

My first marriage. My daughter was not a planned marriage. When she was conceived, I wasn't even married. I was actually engaged to my fiancée, Anne. I was seduced one night to my first wife, and of course, my penis had no conscience, and it got myself into some expensive trouble. This was my fault; so stupid I was. I believe I was set up so she could reel me in. Well, she did. I was old school and thought to be responsible for your actions. So at this time, I called off the engagement with my Italian girl. We were very happy together. My guilt about this baby was killing me. I made one of the biggest mistakes. I broke off the engagement and went to Elkston, Maryland, to get married in her eighth month of pregnancy. We had the baby and went on with our lives. Unfortunately, she was an insecure, jealous person. We would always be fighting and screaming. Eventually, we got divorced. I then would see my daughters on weekends. I would be dating woman, and my ex-wife would always pick a fight with them. Finally, as time went on. I met my second wife. This was a major problem for my ex-wife and my daughter. The problem was my daughter wouldn't accept her because she thought I would go back to her mom. Also, my ex-wife would believe this also. Well, this would never ever be a possibility. So my daughter's hatred grew toward my second wife to this day.

Chapter 8

Life During Second Marriage

I just had enough. I decided to sell my business again. I had a beautiful house, and I also had another rental property. I would sell everything and move down the Jersey shore with a lagoon in the back of my house with a boat.

Well, luck was upon me. I first sold my house at the top of the market. I sold it about ten thousand dollars less than my asking price. I then moved into my rental property until the fish business was sold. I found a buyer; he was very anxious. These buyers are all overwhelmed with the profit and sales numbers. They don't take into consideration you need to work and work hard for it. They are in their own little dream world that every day, they would just pick money off tree branches. I would take weekend trips to the shore looking for my dream house. It was not easy. My main concern was I did not want to deal with greenhead flies and mosquitoes. When I was a kid, my father had a summer home for our family in Beach Heaven West, and the green heads were unbearable. Our arms and legs would swell up from all the bites. So I was on my guard to find the right area. I wouldn't ever want to face that again. We finally found the house. It was beautiful. It wasn't exactly ready to my specifications. We moved in and did the additional work later. I finally finished my training period with the new buyer and moved down the shore completely. I then had time to concentrate on my additions. I had to make it the best on the block. My way of showing off. I put the Belgium block curbs, paver driveway, and walks. A built inground swimming pool, extensive landscaping with manmade stone fountains—one going into the pool, another in the front of the house. The fancy chandeliers and interior and exterior lighting, all granite countertops, imported furniture from Italy. You name it, I had it. The neighbors were stunned especially that they heard I was in the wholesale seafood business and Italian background.

Time went on, and my daughter graduated high school. She needed a place to live. She was going to attend college in Ocean County. She moved into my house. She and my second wife did not see eye to eye. So my wife decided to go to Brazil. This was where she was from. She took our little boy with her. Well, she did not want to come back after that. She and my son grew accustomed to the hot climate and different lifestyle. I then decided I wanted to try to live out there. I was going to open a business and live out there. That would mean I would have to sell my partnership out again. I was not sure it was going to work out there. I wasn't sure I can have a life out there. I was going to open a business and live there. I did not want to sell my personal house or any of my rental properties. I was going to have my nephew manage them while I was out there. I sold my partnership to my good friend Rich, who was also my partner's first cousin. I mentioned him earlier in the book. He knew the business was very profitable. He was out of work, and now he wanted to get involved. I was now free again. I had gone to Brazil to look around, to see what I can possibly do out there. Well, there was a super major shopping mall under construction. It was going to be the mother of all malls in the state. Well, a friend of mine had a pretzel franchise in New Jersey. They had three locations in one mall. He was involved with his brother, and his father was basically retired. These guys had some business. They were always busy. They were making all kinds of money even after the high mall rent and all the franchise fees. The thought came to my mind. How about pretzels in Brazil? Well, I did some investigation, and there was another pretzel franchise out there in many different states. They actually had one that was in a mall that was close to me years ago. It closed down. So pretzels did work in Brazil. I then contacted the same franchise my friend was dealing with. I told them my intentions and what I wanted to do. They were excited to be able to open in another country. I then submitted a business plan to them. They accepted it and told me I would need to open up five locations. I would need to pay for all five up front. There was a training program for two weeks out in California, where their headquarters were located. I went out there, learned the business, and got my franchise certification. I then came back to New Jersey and got some more practice in my friend's store. I then ordered equipment from the United States and items from the franchise to ship to Brazil by cargo ship.

Well, at this time, Brazil was the most corrupt country in the world. I had this cargo leave from Miami, Florida. I hired a freight forwarder to do all the shipping. To make a long story short, his connecting company in Brazil was so corrupt, and between the federal agents in the Port of Santos, Brazil, there was a big mess. To this day, I can't get the true story. My cargo was seized, and I couldn't do any-thing about it. I even went out to the port with a Brazilian lawyer to try to resolve it. Well, my equip-ment was gone, all my baking products gone. Well, I had to search for similar equipment in

Brazil to get the store open. We had opened up two locations in two different malls. The workforce and thinking is very different there. It was such a rigged system for the employees' benefit. I was paying them for everything, their lunch, their transportation back and forth to work. Every week was a holiday or a work strike. It was the craziest situation. They were only allowed by labor law to work one Sunday out of the month. They were not allowed to work overtime. So I was in the mall. My busy days were Saturday and Sunday. The week was slow. So on Saturday, I was shorthanded because they couldn't work more hours, and on Sunday, I was scrambling to find help to work. Then during the week, I had employees looking at each other because it was slow. The inflation would go up every week. The currency was very volatile. Everything would skyrocket. I couldn't keep raising the prices or they wouldn't buy. The vendors just didn't care about their customers. They would deliver when they wanted to. They would try to cheat you on weights, prices, etc. You really had to be alert and on the ball. Between the vendors and the employees ripping you off, it was challenging. I had a camera system, and they still found ways to steal. Even the shopping mall would try their best to screw me. They would give me an exorbitant electric and water bill with no meters to read my usage. I would ask them how they got that figure, and they would ignore me. I proved to them what they were doing was against the law and I was not going to pay until they fixed the situation. I put a lot of time, hard work, and suffering. The laws out there prohibit you from firing or screaming or any loudness to an employee. Well, that didn't work too well for me, dealing with a bunch of ignorant, slow-paced idiots. My Italian descent was always speaking loudly, speaking with my hands, and nervousness didn't help the situation. Every week, I had another employee lawsuit against me. Well, this situation was going nowhere. Every morning, I was leaving my house early, driving all over the city and state with no one to ask directions from or a GPS available. I was shopping at different wholesale warehouses buying supplies. I would also go to the wholesale fruit and vegetable market. That was a blast trying to find the correct products and bargaining for the right prices. Total aggravation, no profit, and the losses were adding up. I finally heard something about my equipment and supplies I shipped from Florida to the port of Santos, Brazil. They were having an auction. It was now two years later. Well yes, you guessed it. I had to bid and buy my own equipment back. Well, if this wasn't the biggest rip-off, what was like a mafia-controlled port. If you remember earlier in the book, when Dad got his special shrimp stolen and had to buy it back from the gangsters, this was a very similar story, but I was dealing with the Brazilian government. I finally had it. I made a decision to get the hell out of there ASAP. I closed down the business, paid everyone, and sold off what I could. Well, after all was said and done, it was quite an expensive learning experience. I took a nice bath… and not with water.

Trips Made Visiting Suppliers

Los Angeles, California

I and my friend Ted took a fish business trip to Los Angeles. He would always be up for going along with me. I always paid his way. He always had a great time, so he always would take the trips. We went out there to meet one of my suppliers and friend Gary. Well, the highlight of this trip was we had entered an LA nightclub dressed like two guidos with gel in their hair and their disco outfits like we were back in New Jersey. Well, that didn't go over too well. We were not accepted by any of the hot women. We were laughed at by the guys after seeing us getting turned down by the woman. Well, we left and figured it out. The next morning, we took a trip to Rodeo Drive. We bought expensive boots and clothes like the locals wore. That night, we went to a different club. Jackpot, we scored a couple of hotties. The new costume paid off. Great trip.

Portland, Maine

It was a very nice fishing port, a very quiet, quaint little village. We went searching for the hot nightclubs, but unfortunately, there were not many to choose from. Quiet trip.

Provincetown, Massachusetts

This was one of the funniest trips with Ted we experienced. We went to see one of the fish suppliers in the middle of the summer. There were a lot of vacationers there. Ted spotted a nightclub from a distance. It was packed solid from a distance. I followed him. He was way ahead of me. It was a very hot day. He took his shirt off. I believe he had a Guinea tee on while walking through the crowd to get in the club. Ted was a very handsome, well-groomed guy. I finally caught up to him. He was surrounded by all these guys. I looked at him. He looked at me. We were in the middle of a gay club. We ran out of there like a bat out of hell. We couldn't believe we ended up there. We totally forgot Provincetown was the gays' getaway place. It was funny as hell. I have taken many trips myself or also with my girlfriend. I was really into having strong relationships with my suppliers. I have taken many trips to Rhode Island, Connecticut, Boston, and New Bedford visiting clam and fish suppliers. I even flew out to Canada and rented a car, driving through wooded areas to visit suppliers throughout the area of Nova Scotia. I had been to Maryland and Virginia, visiting crab and oyster suppliers. I had been in Texas to see my red snapper and grouper suppliers. I actually rented a car in Texas and was driving at a fair speed and was cut off, and a gun waved at me. I then learned that carrying a gun in Texas is legal. Basically, I was told, "Don't piss anybody off." I also was invited down to Mississippi to visit a group of shrimp processors. I have been to Florida to see many suppliers.

Chapter 9

Beginning of Final Seafood Adventure

Well, I packed up with the family. We went back to our house in South Jersey. Thank God I didn't sell anything. I still had my personal house and rental properties. We settled in the house and back to the life I was accustomed to. The guys at the fish business heard I was back. My original partner was having a lot of problems. His cousin was not working out the way he expected. It was a disaster. There was a lot of fighting between them. There were also two other partners, who were not much help either. He asked me to come back because it was too much for him. He was doing all the work and couldn't even take time off. That would make me the fifth partner. I told him I didn't think this was a good idea, five partners. He really needed my help. Well, he didn't have to twist my arm to much especially after I lost a bundle of money in Brazil. I then joined the company again with a small stake and salary.

I really turned the company around. The quality of fish improved. There was a lot less pressure on my first partner. He was able to relax and work some normal hours and go on vacations. I brought in some major accounts. The business more than doubled. It had been five years, and it kept getting busier. At this point, I got back what I had lost in Brazil. I had built up quite a nest egg. My original partner and one of the other partners and I were the only three that were producing. As far as my partner saw it, they were dead wood. They had to go. My partner decided to cut their paychecks in third. Hopefully they would get the message and voluntarily leave. Well, they didn't; they just rebelled. They believed they were doing their job. One of them would be sleeping and snoring in his chair. The other would be texting and eating clams and oysters all day. Well, the bottom line was it ended up in a bloodbath.

Six months later, we finally came to an agreement to buy both of them out. They were both gone. You would never notice a difference. We then decided to move out of our outdated warehouse and into a state-of-the-art, updated refrigerated building. Yes, this was the big leagues. It was all ready. We moved in. We were ready to double our business with this wonderful facility. Well, the fun just didn't stop. Our multimillion-dollar business just turned into a cemetery. With one flick of a switch one morning at 11:30, our world just crumbled into pieces. We were all stocked up with product, fresh and frozen, and then the bomb was dropped. The coronavirus had hit New Jersey bad. All restaurants and food establishments were to close till further notice. Well, that changed things quickly. We had to make some fast, smart, and wise choices. I had the most experience at this. I felt some dangerous roads ahead, but I was preparing for a bumpy ride. The first thing we had to do was cut down on all major expenses. It started from the most expensive employees, our manager, the bookkeeper, fish cutters, and some drivers. We then took seven trucks off the insurance. We stopped purchasing seafood only to a bare minimum. We cut expenses down as far as we could. The first couple of days were scary. There were very few orders. As each day went on, there were more and more orders. People were doing takeout orders. Still, it was nothing close to what it was. That first week, we had so much fish we had to move it out. I pushed and pushed where I could. The wholesale markets plummeted like the stock market. It was a buyers' market. Nobody wanted fish. Unfortunately, we couldn't take advantage of the buying opportunities. The importers and fishing boats took major losses that week.

The following week changed drastically. The importers didn't import any fish products, and the boats stayed tied up at the docks. Fish became scarce, and what was around went up in price. Most of the fish in the United States came from other countries. Overseas, some of the companies had shut down, and also, most air flights were suspended. Air freight rates went up over a dollar a pound. Well, my feeling of possible failure was over. We were doing what needed to be done for survival. We had to make some painful decisions, but it was all about survival. The strong would live, and the weak would float out to sea. I brought my expertise to the show. I performed first class in my occupation. It was all about confidence, knowledge, and power. I took many chances. If I was correct, 80 percent of the time, we were doing good. I had a feel for the market fluctuations and supplies that were available. Also, it was not only that. It was about procuring product. You just didn't call up ABC Company and place an order. Fish was scarce and sometimes nonexistent. It was the relationships you had with your suppliers. Every one of them had a different personality. You need to adapt to each one and be able to be flexible and sometimes let them be in command. It took fifty years to develop relationships with some of these guys. I have visited them. I have built friendship and, most of all, trust. Some of these guys, I have dealt with their fathers and even grandfathers. They also have dealt with my father. Some of them can tell you when I was a little boy walking with my father in Manhattan's Fulton Market. This fish business has been very good to me. It has brought me up to the sky. It has saved my ass. I just want to be very clear with all my readers. I did not inherit anything from my dad while he was alive or even when he passed. He did not start me off in business. He actually made it challenging and hard for me to succeed. If you remember, earlier in the book, he didn't even want to teach me how to cut fish. He was afraid his fish would get destroyed. Can you imagine back then, bluefish was twenty cents a pound and Georgia bank flounders were a dollar a pound? That was dirt cheap. What would he do in today's world, with bluefish a dollar fifty a pound and geo flounders four dollars a pound? Also, I tried to build up his business with wholesale accounts, and he refused to provide me with the correct information. To top it off, he actually threw me out physically out of his store.

Well, I said all the bad things about him. It seemed that I was very upset with him, that I was revolting against him by writing all this. That was not really the case. I needed to get the facts out there. Let's talk about the good things. God rest his soul. I wish he were here to see all my accomplishments. The things he said would never happen or couldn't be done. He actually thought I was crazy. Before he passed, he did see some things about me. I was in business at the age of eighteen, and I was successful. I had bought a building with a mortgage at a very young age. I was purchasing trucks and equipment on credit. I had a brand-new El Dorado Cadillac. I am glad he at least saw this part of my life. I knew he was proud of me deep down inside. I wish he were alive to see his grandchildren and now great-grandchildren and enjoy my house and boat down the shore. Before he passed, my mother and I were talking to him to sell his business and come work with me. This would try to keep him out of trouble. We never had that chance to complete the conversation. His time was up, and with his stubbornness, I didn't even know it that would work. He was sick; gambling is a serious problem. It's possible things could have changed. Well, I owed it all to him to drag my ass out of bed at a young age and train me for life. I also had household chores as a kid. I did receive an allowance. I was not a spoiled kid. If I wanted something expensive, I needed to save up with my allowance or money I earned on Saturdays. This was good, very good. I learned what it was to earn a dollar. If I broke something, I paid for it. If I was bad, I caught a beating. I had the fear of God in me. This was good. I knew my boundaries—what I could do and couldn't do. I knew some things were off limits. Don't even take that chance of doing wrong, may it be in school or at home. I just wouldn't even want to see the consequences.

My mom is a sweetheart. God bless her. She is still living. God is watching over her. She has been through a lot in her life as a young girl growing up in America with her mom and dad, both immigrants from Sicily not able to speak English. She was the baby of the family with many children. She was a survivor of cancer, raising four children, two of which were boys that did give her peace, and a demanding husband, who was not an easy person, who had to have a homecooked meal each day. Later on in his life, he became very bad for her. He was very abusive and disrespectful. He was under pressure with his gambling abuse. He devastated her by losing all their life savings. He cashed in all his insurance/annuities. She would get on him because there were her children she still had to raise and support. She was thinking about the future, the college educations for the children, how they would survive in their older age, etc. It is hard for me to write this, but truth is truth. My dad gave my mom a few whacks sometimes when she would scream at him for his disgraces. My mom was wonderful. She made sure all her children had every opportunity there was from ice skating, horseback riding, music lessons, etc. She provided the opportunity for us to go to college to further our education. Both my parents were very good in their ways. Dad caused some embarrassment to me as a kid. At all my sporting events or other events, Dad did not show. Work came first. All the other dads were there except mine. When Dad passed, I was very sad. I would always tear up or cry if I thought about some moments we had. I am a very emotional person. It's not very macho to be like that, but that's me. I kiss my children and show them affection. I never, ever saw my dad cry or tear up. I don't remember him ever kissing me when I was a kid. He was a very coldhearted guy. He was responsible, hardworking, and a good provider for his wife and children. His ways were a little different, but he kept to himself. He did not have many friends that I knew of in his adult life. I believe and there are others that would also say he was not happy with his life. I believe in the beginning of his marriage and when the first two kids were born, he was happy. As time went on, he lost interest. This is common with most marriages, especially when they were players in their younger age. Their appetite is always there.

I am currently still in the business. I am ready to retire from the seafood business and sell off all my real estate investments. I just hope my health holds out so I can enjoy the rest of the fourth quarter of my game. I hope you found my book interesting and learned about the good, the bad, and the ugly of the wholesale seafood business, how it was, and how it changed. How there is always hope and no one should give up. When things are down, don't be down with them. Keep your head up high, and keep fighting. You need to have a plan and follow it. It's a roadmap to your destiny. Nothing is impossible. When you are on top, don't let it go over your head. Respect everyone and don't throw it in the unfortunate's face. Respect your money. Learn the value of it. As fast as you have it, it can leave you faster. Remember, greed is good, greed is great, but greed will kill you. Thank you, everyone, and God bless you.

This page is dedicated to my very good friend and previous supplier. He passed away several years ago. His name was Joe G. He was an immigrant boy who came over with his family from the Azores. This was a Portuguese-controlled island. Joe was an incredible guy. He never stopped working and worked very hard. The words *failure* and *no* did not exist in his vocabulary. I knew this guy through his good times and his bad times. This guy had a heart of gold. He would do anything for you. His family didn't quite understand his ways completely. He had a confusing life being married twice and having children with both wives. That was still not enough. He was a player; he enjoyed his woman and the white. He was your typical Portuguese greenhorn from the fishing ports. He would have his expressos with shots of brandy. He would frequent the Portuguese sports club. He had an unbelievable personality; he was not shy about anything. Everybody knew him, some people liked him, and some people just wanted nothing to do with him. I met Joe back in the eighties when he opened his first business. We became very close. I was one of his top customers. Well, that business didn't last; it closed down. He then went to work for another company. We were still in contact. Joe would do a lot of side business if you know what I mean. I would take whatever he had. I helped him out to gather capital to open his new venture. He opened up again. He would come down to New Jersey with his young girlfriend, and my girl and myself would meet him in Atlantic City. Those were the days; we would party like crazy. We would take trips to Massachusetts each year and go to different islands on the cape. Joe would bring bags of lobsters and clams, and we would have an old-fashioned clam bake at his house every year. Joe was not a straight arrow guy. He caught himself in trouble with the law. Most of the big guys on the waterfront in New Bedford were not right. They were all fugazy. They did not follow any laws. They made their own laws and had no fear of anything. Joe was in and out of jail. The last time he was in some big trouble, tax evasion. This was a very popular charge on the waterfront. He was away for some time.

Here is one of his funniest stories he told us. He had all kinds of cash stashed in his ceiling. When he was released from jail, there were some bad guys that had a feeling Joe had money put away. One early morning, these guys bust into his house with guns and demanded Joe to give them his money.

Joe replied, "There is no money."

They didn't buy it. They started giving him a bad beating and demanded the money. He was hurting so bad he lost all control of his functions. His eyes started staring at the ceiling. One of the robbers caught on in a matter of minutes; it was incredible. They ripped out all his ceilings in his house. There it went—bags of cash spilled out of the ceiling. The robbers took the cash, and they were gone. Joe was now completely broke. Joe's life turned real bad. His wife left with their child. Joe had no job, no money. We had lost contact. Last year, I asked someone from New Bedford, Massachusetts how Joe was. He told me he had passed. I was very sad. Another legend was gone.

I would always remember one of his famous actions when he was mad with you or didn't want to talk anymore. He would say, "Do you know what I like about the phone?"

You would be dumbfounded and answer him, "What?" He replied and hung up. Then he would slam the phone in your face. That was good ole Joe for you.

Chapter 10

Dishonors

There was one thing that kept me wondering when we had moved into our new house when I was a kid. I was just a young, innocent kid. I didn't know how the system worked, honestly and dishonestly. Well, our new in-ground Anthony swimming pool was installed and ready to be filled. Our neighbor two doors down also had a pool. Well, this big, red fire truck pulled up to our house. All the neighbors and myself were in amazement. Where was the fire? Everyone was wondering. Well, the firemen were hooking up hoses to the fire hydrant and many more extensions to our pool. I never saw this at our neighbor's house. Our pool was getting filled up by the fireman on the city's water. Wow, this was big. No one could say anything. This task was ordered by the mayor, who was also my father's lawyer and personal friend. That was one of the many childhood secrets that was not to be repeated. When we were kids, we would go with Dad on Sundays to get his black Cadillac washed and waxed on Bloomfield Avenue. We would stop by the store to check to make sure there were no problems with any of the machinery. Then sometimes, we would visit some of the customers with envelopes. We would proceed into the country clubs or restaurants and go to the chef's private office. Very discreetly, this envelope would be given to the chef. When us kids got older, Dad gave this chore sometimes to us. Another one was at his fish store. Every fourth Friday of the month, this speech-less, expressionless man in a green uniform who worked for the water company would enter the store and signal my father. He would proceed downstairs with a wrench and do his thing with the water meter. He would then come upstairs, pick up his bag of fresh-cut Georgia bank flounder, and receive a handshake with a coating of cash. This was another story wherein my eyes and mouth would have no motion.

Another fish store story was about the town health inspector. Not that Dad really was indebted to take care of him. Dad kept an immaculate clean, spotless store. People would come from all over and compliment him that there were no flies and the store didn't smell of stinky fish. He was a stickler on this, coming from old nasty fishing boats. You would never believe how clean and orderly this fish market was. This was one of the reasons his business was so successful. Besides all this glamour, just for all purposes, what the hell was a few pounds of fish for the inspector two or three times a month? He was a nice guy and spoke highly of Dad's store. Better to have him on your team.

One of the last fish store stories I will tell for now is about the famous meter maid. Well, the back parking lot was limited on spots and had metered parking. Dad's employees had to park all day and sometimes couldn't run out and feed the meter. Also, some of his top customers would get tickets. Well, there was a fix for all that. It was Manhattan clam chowder. She would stop by whenever and had her unlimited pints of soup when she wanted. At this point, I guess there was a price for everything. This was how business was done in the day. Well, a few years later, Miss Meter Maid left the job. Her replacement didn't like clam chowder. She enjoyed giving more and more tickets out. Well, one day, she couldn't give any more tickets out because her little motor scooter couldn't move. It had received three slashed tires from a 1706 Dexter fillet knife. She was pissed; she called the police, and there was a full neighborhood investigation. Well, they found somebody to confess. The rat, we believe, was from the laundromat. He said it was someone from the fish store. Everyone from the fish store consisted of my brother, cousin Steve, and a fish worker Joe (Stunz). I was not there, thank God. They were all ordered to go into a lineup, and they would be picked out if identified. Well, all three took precautions. Either they didn't shave or got haircuts. My brother sure didn't need a police record going into a top Ivy League college. The witness couldn't identify or didn't want to because he knew his tires would be slashed if not more. The case was over. Our new meter maid liked stuffed flounder. So once again, everything had its way of working out.